The Creative Curriculum® *for* Preschool

Teaching Guide

featuring the Balls Study

Kai-leé Berke, Carol Aghayan, Cate Heroman

TeachingStrategies® · Washington, D.C.

English editing: Lydia Paddock, Jayne Lytel
Design and layout: Jeff Cross, Amy Jackson, Abner Nieves
Spanish translation: Claudia Caicedo Núñez
Spanish editing: Judith F. Wohlberg, Alicia Fontán
Cover design: Laura Monger Design

Teaching Strategies, Inc.
P.O. Box 42243
Washington, DC 20015

www.TeachingStrategies.com

978-1-60617-383-1
Library of Congress Cataloging-in-Publication Data

Berke, Kai-leé.
   The creative curriculum for preschool teaching guide featuring the balls study / Kai-leé Berke, Carol Aghayan, Cate Heroman.
      p. cm.
   ISBN 978-1-60617-383-1
   1. Education, Preschool--Activity programs. 2. Teaching--Aids and devices. 3. Balls (Sporting goods) I. Aghayan, Carol. II. Heroman, Cate. III. Title.
   LB1140.35.C74B45 2010
   372.139--dc22
                              2010002152

1 2 3 4 5 6 7 8 9 10   17 16 15 14 13 12 11 10
        Printing   Year Printed

Printed and bound in United States of America

Acknowledgments

Many people helped with the creation of this *Teaching Guide* and the supporting teaching tools. We would like to thank Hilary Parrish Nelson for her guidance as our supportive Editorial Director and Jo Wilson for patiently keeping us on task. Both Hilary and Jan Greenberg provided a thoughtful and detailed content review that strengthened the final product.

Sherrie Rudick, Jan Greenberg, and Larry Bram deserve recognition for creating the first-ever children's book collection at Teaching Strategies, Inc. Working with Q2AMedia, they developed the concept for each book and saw the development process through from start to finish. Their hard work, creativity, patience, and attention to detail shines through in the finished product.

We are grateful to Dr. Lea McGee for her guidance, review, and feedback on our *Book Discussion Cards*. Jan Greenberg and Jessika Wellisch interpreted her research on a repeated read-aloud strategy to create a set of meaningful book discussion cards.

Thank you to Heather Baker, Toni Bickart, and Dr. Steve Sanders for writing more than 200 *Intentional Teaching Cards*, carefully aligning each teaching sequence with the related developmental progression and ensuring that children will receive the individualized instruction that they need to be successful learners. We are grateful to Sue Mistrett, who carefully reviewed each card and added strategies for including all children.

Translating *Mighty Minutes* into Spanish, ensuring cultural and linguistic appropriateness, was no easy task. Thank you to our dedicated team of writers and editors, including Spanish Educational Publishing, Dawn Terrill, Giuliana Rovedo, and Mary Conte.

Our brilliant editorial team, Toni Bickart, Lydia Paddock, Jayne Lytel, Diane Silver, Heather Schmitt, Heather Baker, Judy Wohlberg, Dawn Terrill, Giuliana Rovedo, Victory Productions, Elizabeth Tadlock, Reneé Fendrich, Kristyn Oldendorf, and Celine Tobal reviewed, refined, questioned, and sometimes rewrote our words, strengthening each page they touched.

Thank you to our Creative Services team for taking our words and putting them into a design that is both beautiful and easily accessible. The creative vision of Margot Ziperman, Abner Nieves, Jeff Cross, and Amy Jackson is deeply appreciated.

Our esteemed Latino Advisory Committee helped us continually reflect on how to support Spanish-speaking children and guided us through the development process. Thank you to Dr. Dina Castro, Dr. Linda Espinosa, Antonia Lopez, Dr. Lisa Lopez, and Dr. Patton Tabors.

We would like to acknowledge Lilian Katz and Sylvia Chard for their inspiring work on the Project Approach that has greatly advanced our thinking about quality curriculum for young children.

Most importantly, we would never be able to do this without the visionary guidance of Diane Trister Dodge. Her thoughtful leadership and commitment to young children and their families inspires all of the work that we do at Teaching Strategies.

Table of Contents

Getting Started

Why Investigate Balls?

Children love balls. They play with them in many different ways. They throw them, catch them, kick them, and roll them with seemingly endless delight. Children learn how natural forces, such as gravity and friction, affect the movement of balls, and they enjoy making balls, marbles, and other rolling objects change speed and direction. The universal and enduring appeal of balls is evident in the traditional games children play with them and in the ways they invent their own ball games.

This study shows how to use children's interest in balls to help them explore social studies and science concepts related to the features and nature of balls, and to use skills in literacy, math, technology, and the arts as they investigate.

How do the children in your room show their interest in balls? What do they say about balls?

Web of Investigations

The *Teaching Guide Featuring the Balls Study* includes five investigations through which children explore the balls that fascinate them. The investigations incorporate indoor and outdoor activities about the scientific properties of balls— why they bounce, roll, and move—and opportunities for children to cooperate.

Some of the investigations also include a site visit as well as demonstrations of the use of balls in sports and exercise by family members and friends. Each investigation explores important concepts in science and social studies and strengthens children's skills in literacy, math, technology, and the arts. Expand this web by adding your own ideas.

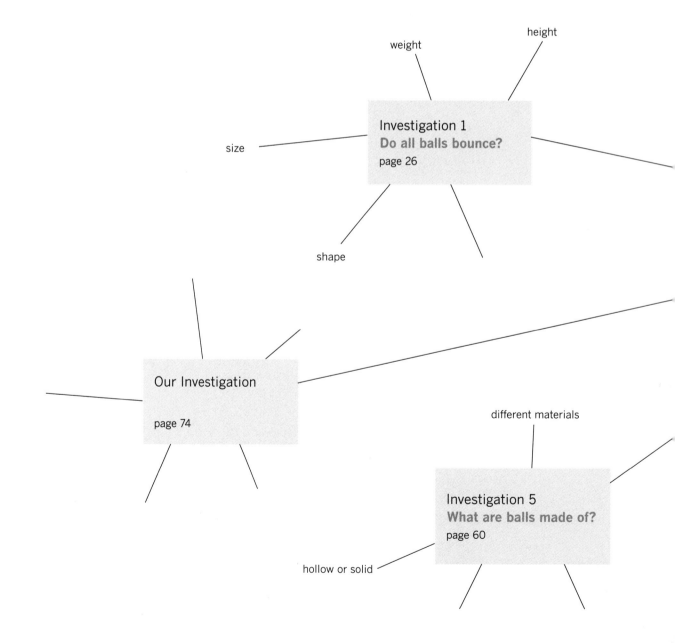

weight

height

size

Investigation 1
Do all balls bounce?
page 26

shape

Our Investigation

page 74

different materials

Investigation 5
What are balls made of?
page 60

hollow or solid

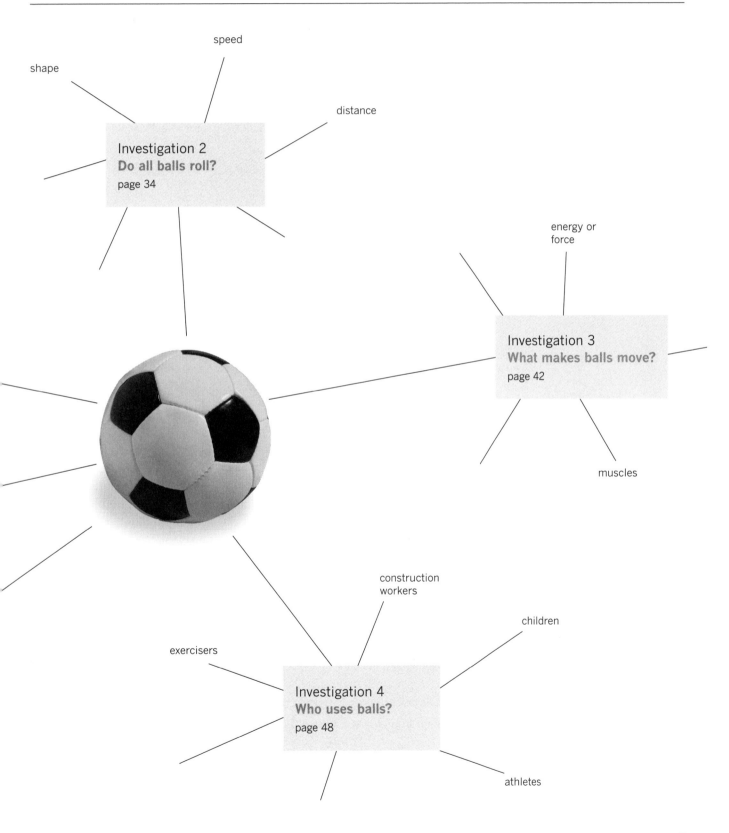

speed

shape

distance

Investigation 2
Do all balls roll?
page 34

energy or
force

Investigation 3
What makes balls move?
page 42

muscles

construction
workers

children

exercisers

Investigation 4
Who uses balls?
page 48

athletes

A Letter to Families

Send families a letter introducing the study. Use the letter to communicate with families and as an opportunity to invite them to participate in the study.

Dear Families,

We have noticed that the children are very interested in balls. They're curious about different kinds of balls, how people use balls, what they are made of, what is inside them, and how high they can bounce. We think balls will make an interesting study.

If you can, we would like your help in gathering a collection of balls to investigate. We'll need many different types of balls. Here's a list of suggestions, but you may also send in balls that are not on the list. We'll take good care of them so we can return them to you at the end of the study.

baseball, basketball, beach ball, bowling ball, cotton ball, crystal ball, doggie	ball, football, golf ball, kickball, Koosh® ball, marble, ping-pong ball, pool (billiard) ball,	racquetball, soccer ball, tennis ball, volleyball, WIFFLE® ball

As we study balls, we will learn concepts and skills in literacy, math, science, social studies, the arts, and technology. We'll also be using thinking skills to investigate, ask questions, solve problems, make predictions, and test our ideas.

What You Can Do at Home

Spend time with your child, playing with balls of all shapes, types, and sizes, such as playground balls, tennis balls, ping-pong balls, Koosh® balls, volleyballs, baseballs, footballs, and marbles. Talk about what the balls are made of, whether they are heavy or light, and whether they are big or little.

Wonder aloud with your child to encourage his or her thinking about balls. For example, you might ask, "I wonder what's inside a tennis ball. I wonder how far you can throw a foil ball, a beach ball, or a tennis ball. How can we find out?"

Help your child use all of his or her senses when playing with balls. You might ask, "What does it look like? Feel like? Sound like? Smell like?"

See how many types of balls you can find around the house and in your neighborhood.

Play a game while riding in the car, bus, or train. Think of all the words that contain the word *ball* in them. Look for examples of balls around you.

At the end of our study, we'll have a special event to show you what we've learned. Thank you for playing an important role in our learning.

Carta a las familias

Envíele una carta a las familias para informarles sobre el estudio. Use la carta para comunicarse y como una oportunidad para invitarles a participar.

Apreciadas familias,

Nosotros hemos notado que los niños tienen gran interés en las pelotas, bolas y balones. Ellos sienten curiosidad por las distintas clases, cómo son usados, de qué están hechos, qué tienen adentro y qué tan alto pueden rebotar. Por eso creemos que un estudio de las pelotas, bolas y balones puede ser interesante.

Para poder realizar nuestro estudio, necesitamos su ayuda para reunir una colección de pelotas, bolas y balones con el fin de investigarlos. Si pueden colaborar, a continuación, les ofrecemos algunas sugerencias, pero siéntanse libres para enviar cualquier tipo que no esté incluido en la lista. Los cuidaremos bien y se los devolveremos al fin del estudio.

balón de baloncesto, balón de fútbol, balón de voleibol, bola de billar, bola de bolos, bola de	ping-pong, bolita (mota) de algodón, bolitas de cristal, canicas, globos, pelota de béisbol, pelota	de golf, pelota de playa, pelota de tenis, pelota Koosh®, pelota WIFFLE®, pelotas para mascotas

A medida que estudiemos las pelotas, bolas y balones, se aprenderán conceptos y se desarrollarán destrezas en lectoescritura, matemáticas, ciencia, estudios sociales, tecnología y las artes. Al mismo tiempo desarrollaremos destrezas de razonamiento investigando, haciendo preguntas, resolviendo problemas, haciendo predicciones y comprobando nuestras ideas.

Qué se puede hacer en el hogar

Pasen tiempo con su niño o niña jugando con pelotas, bolas y balones de todas las formas, tipos y tamaños, como pelotas para jugar en el patio, bolas de tenis, bolas de ping-pong, balones de voleibol, pelotas de béisbol, balones de fútbol y canicas. Hablen sobre el material con que están hechas, si son pesadas o livianas o si son grandes o pequeñas.

Piensen en voz alta para estimular el pensamiento de los niños. Por ejemplo, ustedes podrían decir, "Me pregunto qué tiene adentro una pelota de tenis. Me pregunto qué tan lejos podemos lanzar una bola de papel de aluminio, una pelota de playa o una pelota de tenis. ¿Cómo podemos averiguarlo?"

Al jugar con pelotas, bolas y balones, ayuden a su niño o niña a usar todos los sentidos. Ustedes podrían preguntar, "¿A qué se parece? ¿Cómo se siente? ¿Cómo suena? ¿A qué huele?"

Ver cuántos tipos de pelotas, bolas y balones pueden encontrar en casa y en el vecindario.

Buscar ejemplos de pelotas a su alrededor mientras viajen en el auto, el autobús o el tren.

Al finalizar nuestro estudio, tendremos un evento especial para celebrar lo aprendido. De antemano, les agradecemos su participación y su importante rol en nuestro aprendizaje.

Beginning the Study

Introducing the Topic

To begin this study, you will explore the topic with the children to answer the following questions: What do we know about balls? What do we want to find out about balls?

Begin gathering many different types of balls that you will use throughout the study. Ask the children, their families, and friends to help you build the collection. A sample letter to families is included in the beginning of this *Teaching Guide*.

Build on children's natural interest in balls as your ball collection arrives in the classroom. Think about how to store and display the collection. Make the balls available for children to touch and explore. You probably already have some balls in your classroom and outdoor play area, but consider how to make room for more once the collection begins to grow. You might bring in laundry baskets or a plastic swimming pool to contain the collection. Children are going to be very interested in this growing collection, so make sure they can see the balls easily.

English-language learners
Pay special attention to how children who are not yet proficient in English play with balls so you can verbalize questions based on their actions. "You are rolling different balls down a ramp. What would make them roll faster?" Include the child's name when you speak so that he or she feels included.

Be sure to review the "At a Glance" pages for suggested Wow! Experiences, which require some advance planning.

Here are some suggestions for different kinds of balls to gather.

ball of yarn	crystal ball	marble
baseball	decorative balls	ping-pong ball
basketball	ball-shaped ornaments	pool–billiard ball
beach ball	doggie ball	popcorn ball
bead	football	racquetball
bowling ball	globe	rubber band ball
cotton ball	golf ball	soccer ball
	hollow plastic ball	styrofoam™ ball
	kickball	tennis ball
	Koosh® ball	volleyball
	Magic 8 Ball®	WIFFLE® ball

Preparing For Wow! Experiences

The "At a Glance" pages list these suggested Wow! Experiences, which require some advance planning.

Exploring the Topic:	Day 5: Visit from family members to play ball game
Investigation 3:	Day 1: Visit from family member who plays a sport
Investigation 4:	Day 2: Site visit to a sporting goods store
	Day 3: Visitor with an exercise ball
	Day 4: Visit from a grandparent or older community member
	Day 5: Visitor with a ball-playing pet
Celebrating Learning:	Day 2: Balls Celebration

Exploring the Topic

What do we know about balls? What do we want to find out?

	Day 1	Day 2	Day 3
Interest Areas	**Library:** books about balls **Computer:** eBook version of *The Little Red Hen*	**Toys and Games:** ball collection **Computer:** eBook version of *Have a Ball*	**Toys and Games:** containers to organize the ball collection
Question of the Day	Which is your favorite ball to play with?	Is your ball bigger or smaller than this one (show small ball)?	Is your ball bigger or smaller than this one (show large ball)?
Large Group	**Game:** What's Inside the Box? **Discussion and Shared Writing:** Types of Balls **Materials:** Mighty Minutes 31, "What's Inside the Box?"; box; ball collection	**Song:** "She Brought a Football" **Discussion and Shared Writing:** Share a Ball **Materials:** small ball for comparison; Mighty Minutes 03, "Purple Pants"	**Game:** What's Inside the Box? **Discussion and Shared Writing:** What Can We Do With Balls? **Materials:** large ball for comparison; box with lid; small, nonsports ball; 3–4 different balls; Mighty Minutes 31, "What's Inside the Box?"
Read-Aloud	*The Little Red Hen* Book Discussion Card 05 (first read-aloud)	*Have a Ball*	*The Little Red Hen* Book Discussion Card 05 (second read-aloud)
Small Group	**Option 1: Busy *B*s** Intentional Teaching Card LL16, "Tongue Twisters" **Option 2: Sorting *B*** Intentional Teaching Card LL12, "Same Sound Sort"; collection of items that start with *B*; bag or box to store items	**Option 1: Comparing and Describing Balls** Intentional Teaching Card LL01, "Shared Writing"; ball collection **Option 2: Features of the Ball Collection in Words and Pictures** Intentional Teaching Card LL01, "Shared Writing"; digital camera; ball collection	**Option 1: Laughing Leo** Intentional Teaching Card LL19, "Silly Names"; chart paper; sentence strips **Option 2: Laughing Leo and Dancing Daphne** Intentional Teaching Card LL19, "Silly Names"; chart paper; sentence strips; digital camera
Mighty Minutes™	Mighty Minutes 15, "Say It, Show It"	Mighty Minutes 32, "Walk the Line"	Mighty Minutes 74, "Jack in the Box"

Day 4	Day 5	Make Time For…
Toys and Games: containers to organize the ball collection **Computer:** eBook version of *Have a Ball*	**Toys and Games:** box with lid: interesting collection of small balls **Computer:** eBook version of *The Little Red Hen*	## Outdoor Experiences **Variety of Balls** • Bring a variety of balls outdoors for children to play with and explore. • On day 5, encourage family members to come and play ball with the children.
Does the guessing jar have more or fewer than 10 balls?	How many times can you bounce this ball?	
Song: "Clap a Friend's Name" **Discussion and Shared Writing:** What Do We Know About Balls? **Materials:** Mighty Minutes 40, "Clap a Friend's Name"; ball collection; CD or other flat disk	**Movement:** bouncing a ball **Discussion and Shared Writing:** What Do We Want to Find Out About Balls?	## Family Partnerships • Send home a letter to families describing the study and enlisting their participation. • Invite family members to come and play ball with children during outdoor time. • Invite families to access the eBooks, *The Little Red Hen* and *Have a Ball*. ## Wow! Experiences • Day 5: Visit from family members to play ball with the children outdoors
Have a Ball	*The Little Red Hen* Book Discussion Card 05 (third read-aloud)	
Option 1: Can You Guess? Intentional Teaching Card M17, "Guessing Jar"; large plastic jar; ball collection **Option 2: What's More?** Intentional Teaching Card M19, "Which Has More?"; resealable bags; ice cube trays or egg cartons; collection of small, similar-sized objects	**Option 1: Counting the Collection** Intentional Teaching Card M06, "Tallying"; ball collection; clipboard; paper; pencils or crayons **Option 2: Bounce & Count** Intentional Teaching Card M18, "Bounce & Count"; a variety of balls that bounce; numeral cards	
Mighty Minutes 47, "Step Up"	Mighty Minutes 33, "Thumbs Up"	

Day 1 Exploring the Topic

What do we know about balls?
What do we want to find out?

Vocabulary

English: *examine*

Spanish: *examinar*

See Book Discussion Card 05, *The Little Red Hen* (*La gallinita roja*), for additional words.

Large Group

Opening Routine

• Sing a welcome song and talk about who's here.

> See *Beginning the Year* for more information and ideas on planning your opening routine. Establishing a routine helps all children know what is expected of them. A routine helps children feel comfortable and makes it easier to participate in daily activities.

Game: What's Inside the Box?

• Review Mighty Minutes 31, "What's Inside the Box?" Follow the guidance on the card.

• Use a ball as the object to be placed inside the box.

Discussion and Shared Writing: Types of Balls

• Show the children a few different types of balls. Pass them around, encouraging children to examine how the balls look and feel.

• Ask children to describe the balls.

• Record their ideas.

• Explain, "This week we will study a collection of balls and explore all of your ideas about balls. Let's look at the question of the day and see which type of ball you like playing with best." (The question of the day is located on the "At a Glance" chart.)

Before transitioning to interest areas, describe the books about balls in the Library area and talk about how children may use them.

English-language learners
If possible, include books written in children's home languages. If these are not available, invite family members to make books about balls in their home languages.

Choice Time	As you interact with children in the interest areas, make time to • Read books about balls with children in the Library area. Pay attention to what they find interesting. • Record what they say and do.

Read-Aloud	Read *The Little Red Hen*. • Use Book Discussion Card 05, *The Little Red Hen*. Follow the guidance for the first read-aloud.	• Tell children that the book will be available to them on the computer in the Computer area.

Small Group	**Option 1: Busy *B*s** • Review Intentional Teaching Card LL16, "Tongue Twisters." • Follow the guidance on the card using the following tongue twister: *Barbara blew beautiful bubbles in the big, blue bathtub.*	**Option 2: Sorting *B*** • Review Intentional Teaching Card LL12, "Same Sound Sort." • Follow the guidance on the card using objects that start with the letter *b*. When talking about beginning letter sounds, make sure to include children's names in the activity, e.g., *"Benjamin* and *ball* both start with the /b/ sound."

Mighty Minutes™	• Use Mighty Minutes 15, "Say It, Show It." Follow the guidance on the card.

Large-Group Roundup	• Recall the day's events. • Encourage children who looked at books about balls during choice time to share what they learned or enjoyed about the books. • Invite the children to bring in a ball tomorrow to contribute to the classroom ball collection.	When inviting children to bring in something or do something special for a study, make sure to tell families. Leave them a note on the sign-in sheet, tell them at departure time, or send home a letter.

Day 2 Exploring the Topic

What do we know about balls?
What do we want to find out?

Vocabulary

English: *compound word*

Spanish: *palabra compuesta*

Large Group

Opening Routine

• Sing a welcome song and talk about who's here.

Song: "She Brought a Football"

• Review Mighty Minutes 03, "Purple Pants." Follow the guidance on the card.

• Adapt the song so it is about the kinds of balls children brought to school. For example, sing, "Marie brought a football, she brought a football, picka-packa-licka-lack, she brought a football."

> **Adding new words to a familiar tune helps children learn new songs easily.**

Discussion and Shared Writing: Share a Ball

• Invite children to talk about their balls. Refer to the question of the day as children share their balls.

• Record the names of the balls on a chart.

• Point out compound words as you write them. "The word *football* is made of two words. *Foot* and *ball* are written together without a space between them. When you put two words together to make one new word, it is called a *compound word*."

English-language learners
Combine gestures with words while explaining compound words. For example, when defining *football*, point to your foot and a ball. While helpful to all children, this technique is especially beneficial to English-language learners.

Before transitioning to interest areas, talk about the growing collection of balls in the Toys and Games area and how children can use them.

Choice Time

As you interact with children in the interest areas, make time to

• Talk to the children as they explore the ball collection.

• Record their ideas and questions. Add them to the "What do we know about balls?" and "What do we want to find out about balls?" charts that you will make in the next few days.

Read-Aloud

Read *Have a Ball*.

- **Before you read**, talk about the title. Ask, "What do you think this book is about?"

- **As you read**, take time to talk about the pictures in the book.

- **After you read**, ask, "Were any of the balls in the book the same as the balls that you shared this morning? Which ones?" Tell the children that the book will be available to them on the computer in the Computer area.

Small Group

Option 1: Comparing and Describing Balls

- Review Intentional Teaching Card LL01, "Shared Writing."

- Follow the guidance on the card using the ball collection.

- Invite each child to select a ball from the collection.

- Have each child hold up the ball and describe its features.

- Encourage the children to talk about the texture, size, weight, etc., of their chosen balls.

- As children describe their balls, ask, "How is this different from the last ball we talked about? How is it the same?"

> Save the charts created during small-group time to use on day 4.

Option 2: Features of the Ball Collection in Words and Pictures

- Review Intentional Teaching Card LL01, "Shared Writing."

- Follow the guidance on the card using the ball collection, but take a digital photo of each child as he or she holds the ball.

- Print the photos and attach them next to each child's dictated description of his or her ball.

Mighty Minutes™

- Use Mighty Minutes 32, "Walk the Line."

- Point out how a ball has a curved surface. Follow the guidance on the card.

Large-Group Roundup

- Recall the day's events.

- Ask the children who participated during today's small-group time to recall what they said about the balls they chose.

- Invite the children to bring in another ball tomorrow to contribute to the classroom ball collection.

> Recognition memory gives children a feeling of familiarity when they again encounter something they experienced previously. For example, a child recognizes a book that he or she has heard before. *Recall memory* is harder; children must remember something that is not present, e.g., recall foods eaten by the hungry caterpillar without looking at the pictures.

Day 3   Exploring the Topic

What do we know about balls?
What do we want to find out?

Vocabulary

English: *organize*

Spanish: *organizar*

See Book Discussion Card 05, *The Little Red Hen* (*La gallinita roja*), for additional words.

Large Group

Opening Routine

- Sing a welcome song and talk about who's here.

Game: What's Inside the Box?

- Review Mighty Minutes 31, "What's Inside the Box?" Follow the guidance on the card.

- Use a ball other than a sports ball, e.g., a bead or a cotton ball, for this activity.

English-language learners
While demonstrating what can be done with balls, explain your actions. Children benefit when language is combined with action.

Discussion and Shared Writing: What Can We Do With Balls?

- Ask, "What can we do with balls?" Show the children a few examples to help them get started.

- Record children's responses on a chart called, "What do we know about balls?"

Before transitioning to interest areas, talk about the growing ball collection in the Toys and Games area. Tell the children, "I need you to help me think of a way to *organize* the ball collection today during choice time."

Choice Time

As you interact with children in the interest areas, make time to

- Ask, "What types of balls do we have?"

- Ask, "How can we organize these balls?" If the children need help, ask, "How are some of the balls the same? How are they different? How can these balls be used?"

- Encourage children to sort the balls into categories.

- Recall the question of the day and encourage children to sort the balls by size.

- Record what children say and do.

Provide the children with clipboards and pencils. Encourage the children to sketch the balls they like best as they explore the collection.

Read-Aloud

Read *The Little Red Hen.*

- Use Book Discussion Card 05, *The Little Red Hen.* Follow the guidance for the second read-aloud.

Small Group

Option 1: Laughing Leo

- Review Intentional Teaching Card LL19, "Silly Names." Follow the guidance on the card.

Option 2: Laughing Leo and Dancing Daphne

- Review Intentional Teaching Card LL19, "Silly Names." Follow the guidance on the card.

- Have each child name something he or she likes to do that begins with the same sound as his or her name, e.g., "Tonya likes to tumble."

- Take a photo of each child performing that action. Print the photos and display them with a sentence describing each, e.g., "Daphne likes to dance."

> **Alliteration is the repetition of the initial sounds of two or more neighboring words or syllables. An important part of phonological awareness is learning to hear when words begin with the same sound, such as the /l/ in *Laughing Leo*.**

Mighty Minutes™

- Use Mighty Minutes 74, "Jack in the Box."

- Using the guidance on the back of the card, describe the imaginary box or ball before saying the rhyme.

Large-Group Roundup

- Recall the day's events.
- Invite children who sorted the ball collection during choice time to describe how they organized the balls.

Exploring the Topic

What do we know about balls?
What do we want to find out?

Vocabulary

English: *estimate, sphere*

Spanish: *calcular, esfera*

Large Group

Opening Routine

- Sing a welcome song and talk about who's here.

Song: "Clap a Friend's Name"

- Review Mighty Minutes 40, "Clap a Friend's Name." Follow the guidance on the card.

> When children break down language into smaller and smaller units of sound—from sentences to words to syllables to individual sounds—they are developing phonological awareness. The Clap a Friend's Name game helps children develop an awareness of syllables in a very playful way.

Discussion and Shared Writing: What Do We Know About Balls?

- Say, "We're going to write everything we already know about balls so we can remember."

- Record the children's ideas on the "What do we know about balls?" chart from day 3.

- If necessary, use real balls as prompts to stimulate ideas about what the children already know.

- Begin by recalling some of what the children said earlier in the week, e.g., "Jonathan said you can eat some balls, and Jenna said the beach ball and the basketball are round."

- Hold up a ball and a CD or flat disk. Ask how they are the same or different. Use the word *sphere* to describe a ball.

Before transitioning to interest areas, discuss the ball collection in the Toys and Games area. Recall the different ways the children sorted the balls yesterday.

Choice Time

As you interact with children in the interest areas, make time to

- Invite children to think of a way to organize, display, and categorize the ball collection. Some of the categories might include sports balls, balls used as tools or in machines, decorative balls, balls found in nature, or edible balls. Have children help make the signs for their chosen categories.

Read-Aloud

Read *Have a Ball.*

- **Before you read**, ask, "Who can remember what this book is about?"

- **As you read**, make connections between the balls in the book and those that are in the classroom ball collection.

- **After you read**, encourage the children to find a partner and hunt throughout the room to find one of the balls that is pictured in the book. Tell the children that the book will be available to them on the computer in the Computer area.

> Providing opportunities for children to partner together in games and activities helps them build positive relationships with peers, and practice cooperation and communication skills. Partnering strengthens your classroom community.

English-language learners
Early in the year when English-language learners may be particularly uneasy about participating, pair English-language learners with English-speaking children. They'll feel included and gain oral skills in English when paired with an English-speaking peer.

Small Group

Option 1: Can You Guess?

- Review Intentional Teaching Card M17, "Guessing Jar." Follow the guidance on the card using the jar of balls from the question of the day.

Option 2: Which Has More?

- Review and check children's estimations from the guessing jar activity earlier in the day.

- Review Intentional Teaching Card M19, "Which Has More?" Follow the guidance on the card.

> When offering estimating experiences, begin with numbers just beyond what the children can typically count. For example, offer 3-year-olds collections of 5–10 items, and offer 4- and 5-year-olds between 10 and 30 items.

Mighty Minutes™

- Review Mighty Minutes 47, "Step Up." Follow the guidance on the card.

- Use the chart you made during small-group time on day 2 of this investigation.

Large-Group Roundup

- Recall the day's events.

- Invite children who helped organize the ball collection to talk about the categories they used.

Day 5 — Exploring the Topic

What do we know about balls?
What do we want to find out?

Vocabulary

English: *sphere, tally*

Spanish: *esfera, llevar la cuenta*

See Book Discussion Card 05, *The Little Red Hen* (*La gallinita roja*), for additional words.

Large Group

Opening Routine

- Sing a welcome song and talk about who's here.

Movement: Bouncing a Ball

- Encourage the children to pretend they are bouncing balls with their hands.

- Have them bounce low, high, fast, and slow.

> When you're doing a movement experience with children during a large-group time, it is important to end with a *slow* or *calm* motion. This will help children regulate their behavior and calm down after an active experience.

Discussion and Shared Writing: What Do We Want to Find Out About Balls?

- Post the "What do we know about balls?" chart near the group area so you can refer to it often.

- Say, "We already know a lot of things about balls. Let's think now about what we want to *find out* about balls."

- Prepare a chart called, "What do we want to find out about balls?"

- Model the questioning process for children. For example, you can show them a big beach ball and a small, heavy ball and wonder aloud about their weight. Or show them a ball from the playground that is deflated and wonder aloud what happened to it.

- Record their questions on the chart.

- Help children formulate questions. For example, if a child says, "I think we should make a great big ball," you might say, "You think we should make balls. We'll need to know how to make them. I'll write, 'How are balls made? Can we make balls?'"

- Recall yesterday's conversation about *spheres*. Wonder aloud, "Are all balls spheres?"

- Tell children about the family member(s) coming to play ball with them outdoors.

Before transitioning to interest areas, talk about the "What's Inside the Box?" game that's available in the Toys and Games area. Ask, "How did we play this game during group time earlier this week?"

Choice Time

As you interact with children in the interest areas, make time to

- Observe children playing the game "What's Inside the Box?" Pay attention to their vocabulary. Do they use a variety of adjectives to describe the items in the box?

- Add rich vocabulary to their descriptions. "Michael, you're right. That ball is bumpy. It has a very interesting texture."

> **Vocabulary knowledge is strongly related to later reading achievement. When children learn new words through engaging experiences, they are more likely to remember and use those words.**

Read-Aloud

Read *The Little Red Hen*.

- Use Book Discussion Card 05, *The Little Red Hen*. Follow the guidance for the third read-aloud.

- Tell the children that the book will be available to them on the computer in the Computer area.

Small Group

Option 1: Counting the Collection

- Review the question of the day and talk about the number of bounces. Say, "We just counted bounces. Now we are going to count the number of balls in our collection."

- Review Intentional Teaching Card M06, "Tallying."

- Follow the guidance on the card to count the balls in the collection.

Option 2: Bounce & Count

- Talk about the question of the day.

- Review Intentional Teaching Card M18, "Bounce & Count." Follow the guidance on the card.

Mighty Minutes™

- Use Mighty Minutes 33, "Thumbs Up." Follow the guidance on the card.

Large-Group Roundup

- Recall the day's events.

- Write a group thank-you note to the family member(s) who came to the classroom to play ball outdoors.

Investigating the Topic

Introduction

You have already started lists of children's ideas and questions about balls. As you implement the study, you will design investigations that help them expand their ideas, find answers to their questions, and learn important skills and concepts. This section has daily plans for investigating questions that children ask. Do not be limited by these suggestions. Use them as inspiration to design experiences tailored to your own group of children and the resources in your school and community. While it is important to respond to children's ideas and follow their lead as their thinking evolves, it is also important for you to organize the study and plan for possibilities. Review the "At a Glance" pages for suggested Wow! Experiences. These events require some advance planning.

Do all balls bounce?

	Day 1	Day 2
Interest Areas	**Toys and Games:** sorting trays; a variety of small balls **Computer:** eBook version of *The Three Billy Goats Gruff*	**Toys and Games:** sorting trays; a variety of small balls and circles
Question of the Day	Do you think all balls bounce?	Is your head bigger or smaller than this ball?
Large Group	**Movement:** The Imaginary Ball **Discussion and Shared Writing:** Which Balls Will Bounce? **Materials:** Mighty Minutes 41, "The Imaginary Ball"; ball collection; numeral cards; digital camera; *Play Ball*	**Movement:** The Imaginary Ball **Discussion and Shared Writing:** Height and Bounciness **Materials:** Mighty Minutes 15, "Say It, Show It"; ball collection
Read-Aloud	*The Three Billy Goats Gruff* Book Discussion Card 06 (first read-aloud)	*Bounce*
Small Group	**Option 1: Rhymes With *Ball*** Intentional Teaching Card LL10, "Rhyming Chart"; poem or song with rhyming words; prop that illustrates poem or song **Option 2: Rhyming Zoo** Intentional Teaching Card LL14, "Did You Ever See…?"; pictures of familiar animals; audio recorder	**Option 1: The Long and Short of It** Intentional Teaching Card M25, "The Long and Short of It"; ribbons of equal width, cut into different lengths **Option 2: How Big Around?** Intentional Teaching Card M62, "How Big Around?"; a variety of circular objects; ball of yarn or string; scissors
Mighty Minutes™	Mighty Minutes 30, "Bounce, Bounce, Bounce"	Mighty Minutes 33, "Thumbs Up"; two items with the same initial sound

Day 3	Make Time For...

Toys and Games: add spheres and circles to sort

Computer: eBook version of *The Three Billy Goats Gruff*

Do heavy balls bounce?

Song: Clap a Friend's Name

Discussion and Shared Writing: Weight and Bounciness

Materials: Mighty Minutes 40, "Clap a Friend's Name"; ball collection

The Three Billy Goats Gruff
Book Discussion Card 06 (second read-aloud)

Option 1: Letters, Letters, Letters

Intentional Teaching Card LL07, "Letters, Letters, Letters"; alphabet rubber stamps; colored inkpads; construction paper

Option 2: Buried Treasures

Intentional Teaching Card LL21, "Buried Treasures"; magnetic letters; large magnet; ruler; tape; sand table with sand

Mighty Minutes 37, "Little Ball"; ball

Outdoor Experiences

Bouncing Balls

- Test balls outside to see which balls bounce the highest. Invite the children to make predictions and test them.

- Invite the children to test how balls bounce on different surfaces, e.g., rocks, sand, grass, and concrete.

- If possible, have children test the balls by dropping them from various heights, e.g., slide, steps, and climber.

Physical Fun

- Use Intentional Teaching Card P05, "Throw Hard, Throw Far," and follow the guidance on the card.

Family Partnerships

- Send home a note to families encouraging them to talk with their children about their favorite childhood ball games.

- Invite families to access the eBook, *The Three Billy Goats Gruff*.

Day 1 Investigation 1

Do all balls bounce?

Vocabulary

See Book Discussion Card 06, *The Three Billy Goats Gruff* (*Los tres cabritos*) for words.

Large Group

Opening Routine

- Sing a welcome song and talk about who's here.

Movement: The Imaginary Ball

- Read *Play Ball*.

- Review Mighty Minutes 41, "The Imaginary Ball." Follow the guidance on the card using the numeral card variation.

> An important concept in movement experiences is *body awareness*. This activity helps children explore what their bodies can do.

Discussion and Shared Writing: Which Balls Will Bounce?

- Gather the collection of balls.

- Ask, "Do all balls bounce? I wonder which ones bounce best. Let's find out."

- Hold up each ball and ask, "Do you think this ball will bounce well?"

- Record children's predictions about which balls will bounce, and create two groups: balls they think will bounce and balls they think will not bounce. Let each child test a prediction. Be sure to include some balls that won't bounce and others that don't bounce well, e.g., cotton ball, orange, or football. After testing each ball, have the children re-sort the balls. (They may want more than two categories.) Take photos of children testing their predictions and the sets of sorted balls. Call attention to the football and wonder aloud why it didn't bounce like the others. Reintroduce the term *sphere* to describe balls and point out that the football is not a sphere.

- Say, "I wonder which balls bounce the highest and why some bounce higher than others. During outdoor time today and tomorrow, we can try to find out."

Before transitioning to interest areas, talk about the sorting trays and small ball collections in the Toys and Games area and how children can use them.

Choice Time

As you interact with children in the interest areas, make time to

- Observe children as they sort the balls in the Toys and Games area.

> Instead of praising children by saying, "Good job," encourage children by explaining exactly what they are doing that is appropriate and noteworthy. For more information on this topic see Intentional Teaching Card SE18, "Encouragement."

- Describe what you see children doing, e.g., "You put all the smooth balls in this section and all the bumpy balls in that section."
- Ask, "Can you think of another way to sort the balls?"
- Record what children say and do.

Read-Aloud

Read *The Three Billy Goats Gruff.*

- Use Book Discussion Card 06, *The Three Billy Goats Gruff.* Follow the guidance for the first read-aloud.
- Tell children that the book will be available to them on the computer in the Computer area.

English-language learners
After the reading, retell the story in your own words with gestures. Point to illustrations or objects in the room, as appropriate. This strategy helps children understand the story and learn new vocabulary.

Small Group

Option 1: Rhymes With Ball

- Review Intentional Teaching Card LL10, "Rhyming Chart."
- Follow the guidance on the card using the word *ball.*

Option 2: Rhyming Zoo

- Review Intentional Teaching Card LL14, "Did You Ever See…?" Follow the guidance on the card.

> For more information on supporting children's phonological awareness, see *Volume 5: Objectives for Development & Learning.*

Mighty Minutes™

- Use Mighty Minutes 30, "Bounce, Bounce, Bounce." Follow the guidance on the card.

Large-Group Roundup

- Recall the day's events.

- Show the rhyming chart you made during small-group time. Invite the children to recall rhyming words.

Do all balls bounce?

Vocabulary

English: *circumference, length, shorter, longer*

Spanish: *circunferencia, longitud, más corto, más largo*

Large Group

Opening Routine

- Sing a welcome song and talk about who's here.

Movement: The Imaginary Ball

- Review Mighty Minutes 15, "Say It, Show It." Follow the guidance on the card.

Discussion and Shared Writing: Height and Bounciness

- Talk about the question of the day.

- Briefly recall the previous day's large-group experience about bouncing balls. Show photos from the experience and the sets of balls the children created (balls that bounce and balls that don't bounce).

- Examine the football again and compare it to a sphere. Help children generate ideas about why it didn't bounce well. Help them draw conclusions from their experiences, e.g., "Some of the bouncy balls were big and some were small. Does the size of the ball tell us whether it is bouncy?" Record their ideas.

- Continue exploring bounciness. Encourage the children to make and test predictions.

- Allow one child to stand on a low chair and drop a bouncy ball at the same time that a child standing on the floor drops the same kind of bouncy ball, e.g., a basketball. Ask, "What did you notice about the balls? Which one bounced more? Which one bounced higher? I wonder why."

- Repeat this activity with other types of balls.

- Encourage the children to draw conclusions about height and bounciness. Record their ideas.

> As children make and test predictions and draw conclusions from their explorations, teaching them the right answer is not important. Rather, your role is to support children as they think, question, and investigate engaging concepts by using familiar objects.

Before transitioning to interest areas, talk about the sorting trays and small ball collections in the Toys and Games area and how children can use them.

English-language learners
Include some questions that can be answered in unison with a gesture or a word or two so that English-language learners can participate. For example, while holding up each object, ask, "Which is flat, this CD or this football?"

Choice Time

As you interact with children in the interest areas, make time to

- Observe children as they sort the balls in the Toys and Games area.

- Ask, "How did you sort the balls?"

- Encourage children to sort the collection by two or more features, e.g., "I see you have a pile of smooth balls. Can you sort that pile another way? How about smooth balls that bounce and smooth balls that don't bounce?"

- Record what children say and do.

Read-Aloud

Read *Bounce*.

- **Before you read**, say the title and show children the cover. Ask, "What do you think the dog will do in this story?"

- **As you read**, pause to talk about what the dog is doing in the illustrations.

- **After you read**, invite the children to bounce like some of the creatures in the story, e.g., bunny, frog, bees, and hippo.

Small Group

Option 1: The Long and Short of It

- Review Intentional Teaching Card M25, "The Long and Short of It." Follow the guidance on the card.

Option 2: How Big Around?

- Review Intentional Teaching Card M62, "How Big Around?" Follow the guidance on the card.

Mighty Minutes™

- Use Mighty Minutes 33, "Thumbs Up."

- Follow the guidance on the card using the alliteration variation.

Large-Group Roundup

- Recall the day's events.

- Invite the children who used the sorting trays in the Toys and Games area to share how they sorted the small balls.

Do all balls bounce?

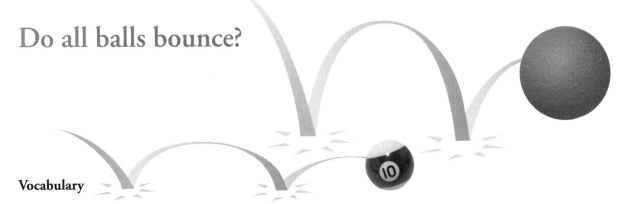

Vocabulary

English: *sphere*

Spanish: *esfera*

See Book Discussion Card 06, *The Three Billy Goats Gruff* (*Los tres cabritos*), for additional words.

Large Group

Opening Routine

- Sing a welcome song and talk about who's here.

Song: "Clap a Friend's Name"

- Review Mighty Minutes 40, "Clap a Friend's Name." Follow the guidance on the card.

Discussion and Shared Writing: Weight and Bounciness

- Gather a collection of heavy and light balls.

- Invite each child to hold a ball and describe its weight.

- Encourage the children to make a prediction about the ball's bounciness.

- Test the predictions and record the findings. Repeat using several other heavy and light balls. Relate this experience to the question of the day.

- Help children draw conclusions about how the weight of balls affects their bounciness.

Before transitioning to interest areas, talk about the new items for sorting in the Toys and Games area and how children can use them.

Choice Time

As you interact with children in the interest areas, make time to

- Listen to how children describe the balls (spheres) and circles in the Toys and Games area.

- Show a sphere and a circle from the collection of items and ask, "Can you tell me how these two objects are the same? How are they different?"

- Record children's responses.

- Use the word *sphere* when describing the round balls.

> *Not* is an important word that is essential to the process of reasoning. Classification skills involve not only what an object *is*, but what it *is not*. Use the word *not* in daily conversations to help children develop reasoning skills, e.g., "These are spheres. These are *not* spheres."

Read-Aloud

Read *The Three Billy Goats Gruff.*

- Use Book Discussion Card 06, *The Three Billy Goats Gruff*. Follow the guidance for the second read-aloud.

Small Group

Option 1: Letters, Letters, Letters

- Review Intentional Teaching Card LL07, "Letters, Letters, Letters." Follow the guidance on the card.

Option 2: Buried Treasures

- Review Intentional Teaching Card LL21, "Buried Treasures." Follow the guidance on the card.

Mighty Minutes™

- Review Mighty Minutes 37, "Little Ball." Follow the guidance on the card.

Large-Group Roundup

- Recall the day's events.
- Invite the children who sorted the circles and spheres in the Toys and Games area to talk about what they noticed about the different items.

- Encourage the children to describe the differences between a sphere and a flat circular object such as a CD.

Investigation 2

Do all balls roll?

	Day 1	Day 2
Interest Areas	Discovery: Basket of 10–20 of the same kind of small ball, e.g., golf balls; a small scale	Blocks: Ramps and balls Computer: eBook version of *The Three Billy Goats Gruff* Intentional Teaching Card SE14, "Playing Together"
Question of the Day	Do all balls roll?	Do you think you could roll a pancake?
Large Group	Poem: "Little Ball" Discussion and Shared Writing: Do All Balls Roll? Materials: Mighty Minutes 37, "Little Ball"; ball collection	Poem: "Come Play With Me" Discussion and Shared Writing: Round Like a Pancake or Round Like a Ball (Sphere)? Materials: Mighty Minutes 42, "Come Play With Me"; play dough or clay; several flat, circular objects
Read-Aloud	*Bounce*	*The Three Billy Goats Gruff* Book Discussion Card 06 (third read-aloud)
Small Group	Option 1: On a Roll Intentional Teaching Card M06, "Tallying"; rolling station or ramp; ball collection; geometric solids of varying shapes; disk-shaped objects; clipboard; paper; pencils or crayons Option 2: Rolling Ramp Intentional Teaching Card M02, "Counting & Comparing"; rolling station or ramp; ball collection; geometric solids of varying shapes; flat disks; card stock; marker	Option 1: I'm Thinking of a Shape Intentional Teaching Card M20, "I'm Thinking of a Shape"; geometric solids; empty containers that are shaped like the geometric solids Option 2: Straw Shapes Intentional Teaching Card M42, "Straw Shapes"; geometric shapes; drinking straws of varying lengths; pipe cleaners; paper; pencils or crayons
Mighty Minutes™	Mighty Minutes 12, "Ticky Ricky"; ball collection	Mighty Minutes 43, "Bouncing Big Brown Balls"

Day 3

Blocks: Ramps and balls

Computer: eBook version of *The Three Little Pigs*

Intentional Teaching Card SE03, "Calm-Down Place"

Can you find something in our classroom that is a sphere?

Game: I Spy…(sphere–circle hunt)

Discussion and Shared Writing: Height and Rolling Balls

Materials: Mighty Minutes 19, "I Spy With My Little Eye"; ball collection; low ramp

The Three Little Pigs

Option 1: Environmental Print

Intentional Teaching Card LL23, "Playing With Environmental Print"; a variety of environmental print; photos of road and store signs

Option 2: Baggie Books

Intentional Teaching Card LL20, "Baggie Books"; 6–8 resealable bags per book; environmental print; construction paper; scissors; stapler; colorful tape

Mighty Minutes 28, "Counting Calisthenics"

Make Time For…

Outdoor Experiences

Rolling Our Bodies

- Encourage children to roll their bodies in a grassy area, on a soft surface or gym mat.

Physical Fun

- Review Intentional Teaching Card P07, "Balloon Catch." Follow the guidance on the card.

Family Partnerships

- Invite a family member who plays a sport to visit the class during Investigation 3, "What makes balls move?"
- Invite families to access the eBook, *The Three Little Pigs*.

Do all balls roll?

Vocabulary

English: *energy, force, gravity, market, shade*

Spanish: *energía, fuerza, gravedad, mercado, sombra*

Large Group

Opening Routine

- Sing a welcome song and talk about who's here.

Poem: "Little Ball"

- Review Mighty Minutes 37, "Little Ball." Follow the guidance on the card, encouraging the children to bounce and roll as you say those words.

Discussion and Shared Writing: Do All Balls Roll?

- Point out to the children that they just made their bodies roll.

- Refer to the "What we already know about balls" chart. If a child had said, "Balls roll," remind the children about that statement. If not, describe a time when you saw a ball roll.

- Ask, "How did we make our bodies roll? What do you think it takes to make balls roll?" Help children notice that rolling an object takes some kind of *force*, such as force from their muscles.

English-language learners

When introducing concepts, it is especially useful to present the words in children's home languages. Say the word in their language and then have the children repeat it in English. English-speaking children also benefit by learning words in a language other than English.

- Refer to the question of the day. Ask, "Do you think some balls roll faster than others?"

- Have several balls available for children to test. Include interesting balls that *don't* roll. Before children roll their balls, have them make predictions.

- Say, "At small group, we will test the balls to see which one rolls the best."

Before transitioning to interest areas, talk about the scale and collection of small balls in the Discovery area and how children can use them.

Choice Time

As you interact with children in the interest areas, make time to

- Observe children as they use the scale.

- Ask questions that encourage children to measure and compare objects:

"Which side is heavier?" and "How many more do you think you'll need to make this side weigh the same as that one?"

- Record what children say and do.

English-language learners

To determine when children need help, especially those who don't yet speak English, look for nonverbal cues: facial expressions, body movements (e.g., a child's turning his or her head to look at you or reaching toward you), or both.

Read-Aloud

Read *Bounce*.

- **Before you read**, ask, "Who can remember what this book is about?"

- **As you read**, pause to let children fill in the rhyming words. Define the words *market* and *shade*.

- **After you read**, look through the book and list all of the balls that children tell you they see. Show the picture of the fruit and ask, "Do any of these fruits look like balls?"

Small Group

Option 1: On a Roll

- Review Intentional Teaching Card M06, "Tallying."

- Follow the guidance on the card.

- Set up a rolling station or ramp that the children can use to test how well various objects roll. Construct the ramp using a board, plank, rain gutter, PVC pipe, or cardboard tube propped securely on a low chair or large block.

- Use a variety of balls and other objects, such as geometric solids, e.g., cans (cylinders), pyramids, boxes (cubes), and flat disks.

- Invite the children to make and test predictions and then sort the objects into categories, e.g., it rolls, it does *not* roll.

- Use the words *gravity*, *force*, and *energy* with the children as they investigate objects that roll.

Option 2: Rolling Ramp

- Review Intentional Teaching Card M02, "Counting & Comparing."

- Follow the guidance on the card.

- Set up a rolling station or ramp that the children can use to test how well various objects roll. Construct the ramp using a board, plank, rain gutter, PVC pipe, or cardboard tube propped securely on a low chair or large block.

- Use a variety of balls and other objects, such as geometric solids, e.g., cans (cylinders), pyramids, boxes (cubes), and flat disks.

- Invite the children to make and test predictions and then sort the objects into categories, e.g., it rolls, and it does *not* roll.

- Use the words *gravity*, *force,* and *energy* with the children as they investigate objects that roll.

Mighty Minutes™

- Review Mighty Minutes 12, "Ticky Ricky." Follow the guidance on the card.

- Use objects related to the ball study.

Large-Group Roundup

- Recall the day's events.

- Invite the children to talk about their experiences at the rolling station during small-group time.

Day 2 Investigation 2

Do all balls roll?

Vocabulary

English: *flat, circular, sphere*

Spanish: *plano, circular, esfera*

See Book Discussion Card 06, *The Three Billy Goats Gruff* (*Los tres cabritos*), for additional words.

Large Group

Opening Routine

- Sing a welcome song and talk about who's here.

Poem: "Come Play With Me"

- Review Mighty Minutes 42, "Come Play With Me." Follow the guidance on the card.

Discussion and Shared Writing: Round Like a Pancake or Round Like a Ball (Sphere)?

- Remind the children about the rolling station they used yesterday during small-group time.

- Give each child a small amount of play dough or clay. Ask, "What could you do to make the clay roll?" Then ask them to make it *flat* like a pancake. Ask, "Can you make your pancake shape roll? Why or why not?"

- Refer to the question of the day. Show the children several flat, circular objects of various sizes made out of various materials, such as CDs, lids, construction paper circles, or a magnetic letter *O*.

- Ask, "Do you think the objects that are round like a pancake will roll?" Record and test their predictions.

- Compare the results to the balls the children rolled the previous day. Help the children draw the conclusion that the objects that are round like a ball or sphere can roll.

> Exploration of two- and three-dimensional shapes is important to the understanding of geometry. Expand children's vocabulary by introducing the correct geometric terms, e.g., "Yes, the ball rolled down the ramp. The ball is a *sphere*, and most spheres can roll."

Before transitioning to interest areas, talk about the balls and ramp-making materials in the Block area and how children can use them.

Choice Time

As you interact with children in the interest areas, make time to

- Encourage children to make and test predictions about rolling balls in the Block area.

- Record what children say and do.

See Intentional Teaching Card SE14, "Playing Together," for ideas on how to encourage children to play cooperatively with others.

Read-Aloud

Read *The Three Billy Goats Gruff*.

- Use Book Discussion Card 06, *The Three Billy Goats Gruff*. Follow the guidance for the third read-aloud.

- Tell the children that the book will be available to them on the computer in the Computer area.

Small Group

Option 1: I'm Thinking of a Shape

- Review Intentional Teaching Card M20, "I'm Thinking of a Shape." Follow the guidance on the card.

Option 2: Straw Shapes

- Review Intentional Teaching Card M42, "Straw Shapes." Follow the guidance on the card.

Mighty Minutes™

- Use Mighty Minutes 43, "Bouncing Big Brown Balls." Follow the guidance on the card.

Large-Group Roundup

- Recall the day's events.

- Encourage children who explored the ramps and balls in the Block area to talk about what they found out.

Do all balls roll?

Vocabulary

English: *fast, faster, fastest*

Spanish: *rápido, más rápido*

Large Group

Opening Routine

- Sing a welcome song and talk about who's here.

Game: I Spy

- Review Mighty Minutes 19, "I Spy With My Little Eye."

- Follow the guidance on the card to help children locate objects in the room that are round like a ball or sphere, and objects that are round like a pancake.

Discussion and Shared Writing: Height and Rolling Balls

- Create a low ramp. Place a ball at the top of the ramp and allow it to roll to the bottom.

- Remind the children of what they discovered in the last investigation about the effects of dropping a bouncy ball from different heights.

- Say, "I wonder what would happen if I raised the top of my ramp higher."

- Make comparisons using words such as *fast*, *faster*, and *fastest*.

- Encourage children to make and test predictions. Record their observations.

Before transitioning to interest areas, talk about the balls and ramp-making materials in the Block area and how children can use them to test their ideas. Say, "I wonder which balls roll the fastest. I wonder which ones roll the farthest."

Choice Time

As you interact with children in the interest areas, make time to

- Encourage children to create ramps of varying heights in the Block area. Ask, "Down which ramp do you think this ball will roll the fastest? Farthest? Slowest?"

- Record what children say and do.

> Some children may become frustrated when exploring new materials or ideas. For ideas on helping children to calm down when experiencing strong emotions, see Intentional Teaching Card SE03, "Calm-Down Place."

Read-Aloud

Read *The Three Little Pigs*.

- **Before you read**, say the title of the book. Ask, "What do you already know about this story?"

- **As you read**, pause occasionally and encourage children to make predictions about what will happen next.

- **After you read**, encourage children to add to the story. Say, "I wonder what that little pig did after the story ended." Tell the children that the book will be available to them on the computer in the Computer area.

Small Group

Option 1: Environmental Print

- Review Intentional Teaching Card LL23, "Playing With Environmental Print." Follow the guidance on the card.

English-language learners
Include environmental print in the languages spoken by children in the class to make them feel welcome and comfortable and to support literacy skills in their home languages.

Option 2: Baggie Books

- Review Intentional Teaching Card LL20, "Baggie Books." Follow the guidance on the card.

Mighty Minutes™

- Use Mighty Minutes 28, "Counting Calisthenics." Follow the guidance on the card.

Large-Group Roundup

- Recall the day's events.

- Encourage children who explored the ramps and balls in the Block area to talk about what they found out.

What makes balls move?

	Day 1	Day 2	
Interest Areas	**Toys and Games:** tools to measure height and circumference **Computer:** eBook version of *The Three Little Pigs*	**Sand and Water:** balls in the water table Intentional Teaching Card SE03, "Calm-Down Place"	
Question of the Day	Which ball game do you like best?	How do you think a ball would move if it were floating in water?	
Large Group	**Song:** "We Like Clapping" **Discussion and Shared Writing:** Sports **Materials:** Mighty Minutes 89, "We Like Clapping"; digital camera	**Movement:** move like water **Discussion and Shared Writing:** The Force of Water **Materials:** Mighty Minutes 34, "The Wave"; instrumental music; scarves, streamers, or ribbons; *The Three Billy Goats Gruff*	
Read-Aloud	*The Three Little Pigs*	*Bounce* light beach balls or balloons	
Small Group	**Option 1: Blow a Ball** Intentional Teaching Card M26, "Huff & Puff"; straws; masking tape; small, lightweight balls; measuring tools **Option 2: Forced Air** Intentional Teaching Card M26, "Huff & Puff"; straws; masking tape; small, lightweight balls; measuring tools; hairdryer or fan	**Option 1: Letters, Letters, Letters** Intentional Teaching Card LL07, "Letters, Letters, Letters"; alphabet rubber stamps; colored inkpads; construction paper **Option 2: Buried Treasures** Intentional Teaching Card LL21, "Buried Treasures"; magnetic letters; large magnet; ruler; tape; sand table with sand	
Mighty Minutes™	Mighty Minutes 35, "My Name, Too!"	Mighty Minutes 33, "Thumbs Up"; familiar three-dimensional objects	

Make Time For…

Outdoor Experiences

Move A Ball

- Explore the different ways balls can move or can be moved from one place to another.

- Challenge children to think of all the different ways they can move a ball from one side of the playground to another without touching, hitting, or kicking it. If possible, experiment with using a leaf blower to move balls across the playground.

- Invite children to make and test predictions.

- Take pictures of their investigation.

Physical Fun

- Use Intentional Teaching Card P07, "Balloon Catch." Follow the guidance on the card.

Family Partnerships

- Invite family or community members to the classroom during Investigation 4, "Who uses balls?"

  - Invite a family member who uses an exercise ball. Alternatively, contact a local gym or athletic center to see whether someone is available to show the children how to use an exercise ball.

  - Invite a grandparent or other older family or community member who can tell a story about a ball game he or she played as a child.

  - Invite a family member and his or her pet who plays with a ball, e.g., a dog that catches a ball or a hamster that plays inside a ball.

- Invite families to access the eBook, *The Three Little Pigs*.

Wow! Experiences

- Day 1: Visit from a family member who plays a sport

Day 1 Investigation 3

What makes balls move?

Vocabulary

English: *energy, force, circumference, height*

Spanish: *energía, fuerza, circunferencia, altura*

Large Group

Opening Routine

• Sing a welcome song and talk about who's here.

Song: "We Like Clapping"

• Review Mighty Minutes 89, "We Like Clapping."

• Follow the guidance on the card using the word *bouncing*.

Discussion and Shared Writing: Sports

• Talk about the question of the day.

• Introduce the family member to the children and tell them what sport he or she plays.

• Ask the family member to talk about the sport, e.g., how she started playing, what he does with the ball in the sport. Ask the family member to demonstrate how the ball is moved in the sport, e.g., dribbled, thrown, or kicked.

• Encourage the children to ask questions. Record their questions and the visitor's responses.

• Say, "In any sport, we need *muscles* to move a ball." Ask the visitor to demonstrate or describe how he or she keeps his or her muscles strong to participate in the sport.

Remember to take pictures of Wow! Experiences, such as visitors to the classroom. Post the pictures with the charts on which you recorded children's discussions. The pictures will encourage them to reflect on their experiences and learning during the study.

Before transitioning to interest areas, tell the children what *circumference* means. Ask a child to help you measure the *circumference* of the visitor's ball using yarn as the measuring tool. Have the child wrap the yarn around the widest part of the ball (at its equator). Cut the yarn so it is exactly the circumference of the ball. Then, have another child measure the ball's *height* with a different piece of yarn. Cut that child's piece of yarn to show the ball's height. Hold the two pieces next to each other, and ask, "Which is longer: the piece that measured the height or the piece that measured the circumference?" Tell children that they can continue experimenting with height and circumference using the ball collection in the Toys and Games area.

Choice Time	As you interact with children in the interest areas, make time to • Observe children as they measure the height and circumference of balls in the Toys and Games area. Offer assistance as needed.	• Ask, "Can you find a ball that is bigger around (*circumference*) than it is tall (*height*)?" • Record what children say and do.
Read-Aloud	Read *The Three Little Pigs.* • **Before you read**, show children the cover and ask, "What is the title of this book?" • **As you read**, pause to let children fill in predictable phrases.	• **After you read**, ask the children what props they would need to act out the story. Record their ideas and then help them gather the props. Tell them that the props and book will be in the Library area for them to use if they wish to act out the story during choice time. Tell the children that the book will be available to them on the computer in the Computer area.

Small Group	**Option 1: Blow a Ball** • Review the story of *The Three Little Pigs.* Talk with the children about the *energy* and *force* of the wolf's blowing. • Review Intentional Teaching Card M26, "Huff & Puff." Follow the guidance on the card.	**Option 2: Forced Air** • Review the story of *The Three Little Pigs.* Talk with the children about the *energy* and *force* of the wolf's blowing. • Review Intentional Teaching Card M26, "Huff & Puff." Follow the guidance on the card. • Extend the children's investigation of forced air by using a fan or hairdryer to provide the energy to move the ball. Have the children select a variety of balls to test while you operate the fan or hairdryer.

Mighty Minutes™	• Use Mighty Minutes 35, "My Name, Too!" Follow the guidance on the card.

Large-Group Roundup	• Recall the day's events. • Write a group thank-you note to the family member who visited the classroom today.	**English-language learners** When expressing themselves, children who are learning a new language may use the new language along with words from their home languages. Combining words from both languages is typical and does not indicate confusion.

Day 2 Investigation 3

What makes balls move?

Vocabulary

English: *force, tip*

Spanish: *fuerza, punta*

Large Group

Opening Routine

- Sing a welcome song and talk about who's here.

Movement: Move Like Water

- Review Mighty Minutes 34, "The Wave." Follow the guidance on the card.

Discussion and Shared Writing: The Force of Water

- Show children the page of *The Three Billy Goats Gruff* with rushing water.

- Talk about how the force of the water was so strong that it carried the troll away.

- Ask, "Do you think water can move a ball?"

- Record the children's predictions.

Before transitioning to interest areas, talk about the balls in the water table in the Sand and Water area. Explain to the children that they will have the opportunity to test their predictions. Talk about the question of the day.

Choice Time

As you interact with children in the interest areas, make time to

- Encourage children to experiment with the balls in the water table.

- Describe what the children are doing and the results of their actions, e.g., "You poured water from the can onto the ball. That made the ball spin in the water."

- Record what children say and do.

For more ideas on engaging children in the Sand and Water area, see *The Creative Curriculum for Preschool, Volume 2: Interest Areas*.

Read-Aloud

Read *Bounce*.

- **Before you read**, cover the title and ask, "What is the name of this book?"

- **As you read**, define the word *tip* by pointing to the tip of your nose.

- **After you read**, provide several light beach balls or balloons and encourage children to experiment with bouncing them on the tips of their noses. Invite them to try to bounce the beach balls on other parts of the body, too, e.g., elbow, knee, and head.

Small Group

Option 1: Letters, Letters, Letters

- Review Intentional Teaching Card LL07, "Letters, Letters, Letters." Follow the guidance on the card.

Option 2: Buried Treasures

- Review Intentional Teaching Card LL21, "Buried Treasures." Follow the guidance on the card.

> **Repeating small-group experiences provides opportunities for children to build on recently acquired knowledge.**

Mighty Minutes™

- Use Mighty Minutes 33, "Thumbs Up."

- Try the shape variation on the back of the card.

Large-Group Roundup

- Recall the day's events.

- Invite children who experimented with the balls in the water table during choice time to talk about what they found out.

Investigation 4

Who uses balls?

	Day 1	Day 2	Day 3
Interest Areas	Toys and Games: three-dimensional shape sort	Blocks: wrecking ball (beach ball tied to a long piece of yarn); cardboard blocks Computer: eBook versions of *Have a Ball* and *Play Ball!*	Dramatic Play: materials suggested during Large-Group Roundup on day 2
Question of the Day	What do you think we will see on our site visit?	Have you ever been to a store that sells balls?	Can you make your body into a ball?
Large Group	Song: I Can Make a Circle Discussion and Shared Writing: Preparing for the Site Visit Materials: Mighty Minutes 23, "Hi-Ho, the Derry-O"; Mighty Minutes 20, "I Can Make a Circle"	Book: *Have a Ball* Discussion and Shared Writing: Questions for the Site Visit Materials: *Have a Ball*; Intentional Teaching Card SE01, "Site Visits"; digital camera	Game: Body Patterns Discussion and Shared Writing: Exercise Ball Materials: Mighty Minutes 36, "Body Patterns"; digital camera
Read-Aloud	*Just Like Josh Gibson* Book Discussion Card 07 (first read-aloud)	*Play Ball!*	*Just Like Josh Gibson* Book Discussion Card 07 (second read-aloud)
Small Group	Option 1: What's Missing? Intentional Teaching Card LL18, "What's Missing?"; ball collection; bag or box; large piece of paper or cardboard Option 2: Memory Card Game Intentional Teaching Card LL08, "Memory Games"; memory game, lotto game, or a set of duplicate pictures or objects	Option 1: Geoboards Intentional Teaching Card M21, "Geoboards"; geoboards; rubber bands; shape cards Option 2: I'm Thinking of a Shape Intentional Teaching Card M20, "I'm Thinking of a Shape"; geometric solids; empty containers shaped like the geometric solids	Option 1: Bead Patterns Intentional Teaching Card M14, "Patterns"; beads; examples of patterns; construction paper; crayons or markers Option 2: Jewelry Making Intentional Teaching Card M14, "Patterns"; jewelry-making supplies, e.g., beads, string, colored straws; construction paper; crayons or markers
Mighty Minutes™	Mighty Minutes 04, "Riddle Dee Dee"	Mighty Minutes 42, "Come Play With Me"	Mighty Minutes 30, "Bounce, Bounce, Bounce"

Day 4	Day 5	Make Time For...
Toys and Games: beads, laces **Computer:** eBook version of *Play Ball!*	**Discovery:** natural spherical items; magnifying glasses **Art:** materials for thank-you notes **Library:** Intentional Teaching Card SE19, "Friendship & Love Cards"	## Outdoor Experiences ### Sphere Hunt • Have the children look for spherical items outside. • Collect or take pictures of the spherical items that the children found. ### Physical Fun • Review Intentional Teaching Card P06, "Catching With a Scoop." Follow the guidance.
What's your favorite thing to do with balls?	What kinds of animals play with balls?	
Song: "Clap a Friend's Name" **Discussion and Shared Writing:** Visiting Grandparent **Materials:** Mighty Minutes 40, "Clap a Friend's Name"; digital camera	**Game:** animal movement **Discussion and Shared Writing:** Pets That Play Ball **Materials:** Mighty Minutes 39, "Let's Pretend"; digital camera; writing materials; paper	## Family Partnerships • Encourage children to interview their families about games they played with balls when they were children. • Invite families to access the eBook, *Play Ball!*
Play Ball! paper; writing materials; Intentional Teaching Card LL32, "Describing Art"	*Just Like Josh Gibson* Book Discussion Card 07 (third read-aloud)	## Wow! Experiences • Day 2: Site visit to a sporting goods store • Day 3: Visitor with an exercise ball • Day 4: Visit from a grandparent or older community member • Day 5: Visitor with a ball-playing pet
Option 1: Sphere Hunt Book Intentional Teaching Card LL04, "Bookmaking"; cardboard or card stock; paper; pencils, crayons, or markers; bookbinding supplies; clipboards **Option 2: Sphere Hunt Computer Book** Intentional Teaching Card LL02, "Desktop Publishing"; digital camera; computer; each child's word bank; printer; paper; bookbinding supplies	**Option 1: Sphere Hunt Book** Intentional Teaching Card LL04, "Bookmaking"; cardboard or card stock; paper; pencils, crayons, or markers; bookbinding supplies; clipboards **Option 2: Sphere Hunt Computer Book** Intentional Teaching Card LL02, "Desktop Publishing"; digital camera; computer; each child's word bank; printer; paper; bookbinding supplies	
Mighty Minutes 28, "Counting Calisthenics"	Mighty Minutes 05, "Silly Willy Walking"	

Day 1 · Investigation 4

Who uses balls?

Vocabulary

English: *cube, rectangular prism, cylinder, sphere, interview*

Spanish: *cubo, prisma rectangular, cilindro, esfera, entrevista*

See Book Discussion Card 07, *Just Like Josh Gibson (Igual que Josh Gibson)*, for additional words.

Large Group

Opening Routine

- Sing a welcome song and talk about who's here.

Song: "I Can Make a Circle"

- Review Mighty Minutes 20, "I Can Make a Circle." Follow the guidance on the card.

English-language learners
When English-language learners respond to the question of the day by using single words or short phrases, expand on their words to help them gain knowledge of English vocabulary and grammar. For example, if a child says, "Baseball," expand the answer by saying, "You think you'll see a baseball at the store."

**Discussion and Shared Writing:
Preparing for the Site Visit**

- Tell the children, "Tomorrow we will be going on a site visit. We're going to a store that sells balls."

- Refer to the question of the day. Ask, "What do you think we will see at the store?"

- Discuss their responses and help the children expand their thinking.

- Record their ideas.

- Review Mighty Minutes 23, "Hi-Ho, the Derry-O." Follow the guidance on the card to sing about the site visit.

Before transitioning to interest areas, talk about the three-dimensional shapes in the Toys and Games area and how children can use them.

English-language learners
Send home a note explaining the interview activity to the families. If family members are not proficient in English, write the note in children's home languages. If necessary, ask colleagues or family members to help with this task.

Choice Time

As you interact with children in the interest areas, make time to

- Ask children to describe the shapes in the Toys and Games area.

- Talk about the three-dimensional shapes using the proper terminology. For example, say, "A *cube* is like a box, a *rectangular prism* is like a long box, a *cylinder* is like a can, and a *sphere* is like a ball."

> **Naming shapes is not the most important aspect of geometry. Providing hands-on experiences, such as a rolling station, helps children learn about the attributes of three-dimensional shapes.**

Read-Aloud

Read *Just Like Josh Gibson*.

- Review Book Discussion Card 07, *Just Like Josh Gibson*. Follow the guidance for the first read-aloud.

Small Group

Option 1: What's Missing?

- Review Intentional Teaching Card LL18, "What's Missing?" Follow the guidance on the card.

- Use several balls from the collection to play the game.

Option 2: Memory Card Game

- Review Intentional Teaching Card LL08, "Memory Games." Follow the guidance on the card.

- Use any memory or lotto game that you have in your classroom. If you don't have one, you can create one by gluing pictures of matching balls onto index cards.

Mighty Minutes™

- Use Mighty Minutes 04, "Riddle Dee Dee."

- Try the variation on the back of the card.

Large-Group Roundup

- Recall the day's events.
- Remind the children that they'll be going on a site visit tomorrow. Ask them what questions they would like to ask the people that work there. Record their ideas.

- Invite the children to interview a family member or neighbor about ball games he or she plays now or played at a younger age.

Who uses balls?

Vocabulary

English: *wrecking ball*

Spanish: *bola de demolición*

Large Group

Opening Routine

- Sing a welcome song and talk about who's here.

Book: *Have a Ball*

- Read *Have a Ball*. Point out the *wrecking ball* in the story. Tell the children that the book will be available to them on the computer in the Computer area.

Discussion and Shared Writing: Questions for the Site Visit

- Talk about the question of the day.

- Review the children's questions from the previous day at large-group roundup time. Ask, "Does anyone have any other questions to ask at the site visit today? Let's talk about them and add them to our chart."

- Remind children about expectations for their behavior before the site visit. See Intentional Teaching Card SE01, "Site Visits," for more information.

Before transitioning to interest areas, talk about the wrecking ball in the protected section of the Block area and how children can use it. Ask, "How can we be safe while we use the wrecking ball? How can we make sure the ball doesn't knock down other buildings in the Block area?" Record their responses. Post their "rules" for safety using the wrecking ball in the Block area.

Use a shelf or other low divider to create a special section for the wrecking ball in the Block area. If this will not work in your classroom, try going outdoors where there may be more space.

Choice Time

As you interact with children in the interest areas, make time to

- Observe children as they use the wrecking ball. Take photos to post in the Block area later.

- Record what children say and do.
- After returning from the site visit, invite the children to write a group thank-you note to the staff members they met there.

Read-Aloud

Read *Play Ball!*

- **Before you read**, talk about the cover of the book.
- **As you read**, take time to point out details in the pictures.

- **After you read**, invite children to talk about any experiences they have had playing the sports and games described in the book. Tell the children that the book will be available to them on the computer in the Computer area.

Small Group

Option 1: Geoboards

- Review Intentional Teaching Card M21, "Geoboards." Follow the guidance on the card.

Option 2: I'm Thinking of a Shape

- Review Intentional Teaching Card M20, "I'm Thinking of a Shape." Follow the guidance on the card.

Mighty Minutes™

- Use Mighty Minutes 42, "Come Play With Me." Follow the guidance on the card.

- Try using one of the variations on the back of the card.

Large-Group Roundup

- Recall the day's events.
- Ask the children to share their experiences from today's site visit.
- Ask, "If we wanted to turn the Dramatic Play area into a place like the one we saw on our site visit, what would we need?"
- Have children refer to the photos taken at the site. Draw their attention to the signs in the store as well as the displays. Record their responses.

English-language learners
Asking some simple questions that can be answered with a single word or by pointing to something in a photograph helps children with little oral language proficiency participate in large-group discussions. For example, ask, "Which ball at the store did you like best?"

Day 3 | Investigation 4

Who uses balls?

Vocabulary

English: *pattern*

Spanish: *patrón*

See Book Discussion Card 07, *Just Like Josh Gibson* (*Igual que Josh Gibson*), for additional words.

Large Group

Opening Routine

- Sing a welcome song and talk about who's here.

Game: Body Patterns

- Talk about the question of the day.

- Review Mighty Minutes 36, "Body Patterns." Follow the guidance on the card.

> Helping children understand what their bodies can do and different ways to move them paves the way for them to enjoy physical activities and a healthy lifestyle in general.

Discussion and Shared Writing: Exercise Ball

- Introduce the visitor to the children. Invite him or her to explain and demonstrate how he or she uses a ball for exercise.

- Encourage the children to ask questions. Record their questions and the visitor's responses.

- If possible, let children try out the exercises using appropriately sized balls.

- Take photos to document the experience.

Before transitioning to interest areas, remind children of the materials they listed yesterday during large-group roundup. Talk about the new choices in the Dramatic Play area (materials to re-create the site they visited) and how children can use them.

English-language learners
Children who are not yet speaking English may find dramatic play one of the most challenging and perhaps stressful classroom activities. Introducing the appropriate props and modeling roles they might play help children feel comfortable about participating.

Choice Time

As you interact with children in the interest areas, make time to

- Build on children's ideas by suggesting ways in which the new materials in the Dramatic Play area can be used. For example, say, "Tanya said you need lots of money to buy this big exercise ball. Why don't we use these stickers to put price tags on everything so customers will know how much things cost?"

- Observe children as they use the new materials in the Dramatic Play area. Relate their play to their experiences at the site visit. Remind children about the roles of the store workers and what they saw customers doing at the store, e.g., "Malik is the customer, and he is paying Alex for the basketball. How much money does the basketball cost?"

- Record what children say and do.

> When children are engaged in buying and selling in the Dramatic Play area, they are learning about economics, a component of the social studies content area.

Read-Aloud

Read *Just Like Josh Gibson.*

- Review Book Discussion Card 07, *Just Like Josh Gibson.* Follow the guidance for the second read-aloud.

Small Group

Option 1: Bead Patterns

- Review Intentional Teaching Card M14, "Patterns." Follow the guidance on the card.

- Have the children make patterns using beads and laces.

Option 2: Jewelry Making

- Review Intentional Teaching Card M14, "Patterns." Follow the guidance on the card.

- Have the children use various items to make jewelry, e.g., small beads and string; a few different kinds of colored straws cut into pieces.

Mighty Minutes™

- Use Mighty Minutes 30, "Bounce, Bounce, Bounce." Follow the guidance on the card.

Large-Group Roundup

- Recall the day's events.

- Remind the children to talk to their families about ball games they play now or played at a younger age.

Day 4 | Investigation 4

Who uses balls?

Vocabulary

English: *pattern*

Spanish: *patrón*

Large Group

Opening Routine

- Sing a welcome song and talk about who's here.

Song: "Clap a Friend's Name"

- Review Mighty Minutes 40, "Clap a Friend's Name." Follow the guidance on the card.

Discussion and Shared Writing: Visiting Grandparent

- Talk about the question of the day.

- Introduce the grandparent, or older family or community member, to the children, or invite the related child to introduce the visitor.

- Invite the visitor to talk about a ball game that he or she played as a child.

- Encourage the children to ask questions. Record their questions and the visitor's responses.

- Take photos to document the experience.

Before transitioning to interest areas, talk about the beads and laces in the Toys and Games area and how children can use them to make patterns. Also, talk about the materials in the Art area to make thank-you notes for the visitor who brought in an exercise ball.

> **If possible, find out in advance what items today's visitor used to play his or her ball game. Plan to have those items available for the children to explore.**

Choice Time

As you interact with children in the interest areas, make time to

- Talk to the children about the patterns they created. Ask them to describe the patterns.

- Take photos of the bead patterns. Display the photos next to the children's dictation.

> **Talk informally about the letters and their sounds as you write them, e.g., "*Red* starts with the /r/ sound. That's the letter *r*. *Rainbow* starts with the /r/ sound, too. Watch how I write an *r*."**

Read-Aloud

Read *Play Ball!*

- **Before you read**, remind the children that earlier in the week you asked them to interview their families about ball games. Invite them to share what they learned.

- **As you read**, relate the ball games in the story to the ones the children mentioned that their family members play.

- **After you read**, give the children time to write and draw about one of the ball games in the story or one that their family members mentioned in the interviews. Record what they say about their work and create a display in the classroom. Tell the children that the book will be available to them on the computer in the Computer area.

> See Intentional Teaching Card LL32, "Describing Art," for more information about recording children's dictation.

Small Group

Option 1: Sphere Hunt Book

- Review Intentional Teaching Card LL04, "Bookmaking." Follow the guidance on the card.

- Tell the children that they will be going on a sphere hunt outdoors.

- Give each child a clipboard with paper.

- Explain that they should look for ball-shaped items. Encourage the children to sketch what they find.

Option 2: Sphere Hunt Computer Book

- Review Intentional Teaching Card LL02, "Desktop Publishing." Follow the guidance on the card.

- Tell the children that they will be going on a sphere hunt outdoors.

- Explain that they should look for ball-shaped items. Encourage the children to take digital photos of what they find.

Mighty Minutes™

- Use Mighty Minutes 28, "Counting Calisthenics." Follow the guidance on the card.

- Try using balls with the exercises.

Large-Group Roundup

- Recall the day's events.

- Invite children who worked on the book during small-group time to talk about the ball-shaped objects they found outdoors.

- Talk about the family member who will be bringing his or her ball-playing pet to visit the class tomorrow. Remind the children that sudden movements and loud noises may scare the animal, so it is important that they use quiet voices and move slowly when the pet is visiting.

> If tomorrow's animal visitor is a dog and weather permits, you may want to plan on having part of large-group time outside. The dog may feel more comfortable with the additional space and will have more room to show how he or she plays with a ball. Check with your program for any rules related to animals visiting.

Day 5 Investigation 4

Who uses balls?

Vocabulary

See Book Discussion Card 07, *Just Like Josh Gibson* (*Igual que Josh Gibson*), for words.

Large Group

Opening Routine

- Sing a welcome song and talk about who's here.

Game: Animal Movement

- Review Mighty Minutes 39, "Let's Pretend." Follow the guidance on the card.

- Try the variation on the back to move like different animals.

Discussion and Shared Writing: Pets That Play Ball

- Review the question of the day.

- Remind the children to use quiet voices and move slowly around the animal visitor so that the animal will feel more secure.

- Introduce the visitor and pet to the children. Invite the visitor to talk about how his or her pet plays with a ball.

- Invite the children to ask questions. Record their questions and the visitor's responses.

- Give the children time to draw a sketch of the animal as they observe it playing with a ball.

> If a child feels nervous around the animal visitor, invite him or her to sit with you or another adult in a different area of the room. Both the child and the animal may feel more comfortable when there is some distance between them.

Before transitioning to interest areas, talk about the collection of natural spherical items in the Discovery area and how children can use them. Also talk about the materials in the Art area that the children can use to make thank-you cards for all of the family members who visited the classroom during this investigation.

Choice Time

As you interact with children in the interest areas, make time to

- Ask the children what they would like to say to the visitor and record their dictation on the thank-you cards.

- Encourage them to write as many words as they can. Have them try to sign their own names on the card.

- Observe children as they explore the collection of natural items in the Discovery area. Offer magnifying glasses so they can get a more detailed look.

- Ask questions to encourage the children to describe the objects. Invite them to document their observations on paper, e.g., draw a picture of what they see when they look at one of the objects through a magnifying glass.

> Since the card-making materials are already available, children may want to make cards for other people as well. See Intentional Teaching Card SE19, "Friendship & Love Cards."

Read-Aloud

Read *Just Like Josh Gibson*.

- Review Book Discussion Card 07, *Just Like Josh Gibson*. Follow the guidance for the third read-aloud.

Small Group

Option 1: Sphere Hunt Book

- Review Intentional Teaching Card LL04, "Bookmaking." Follow the guidance on the card.

- Tell the children that they will be going on a sphere hunt outdoors.

- Give each child a clipboard with paper.

- Explain that they should look for ball-shaped items. Encourage the children to sketch what they find.

Option 2: Sphere Hunt Computer Book

- Review Intentional Teaching Card LL02, "Desktop Publishing." Follow the guidance on the card.

- Tell the children that they will be going on a sphere hunt outdoors.

- Explain that they should look for ball-shaped items. Invite the children to take digital photos of what they find.

Mighty Minutes™

- Use Mighty Minutes 05, "Silly Willy Walking." Follow the guidance on the card.

- Relate this experience to the "Let's Pretend" animal experience that the children participated in earlier.

Large-Group Roundup

- Recall the day's events.

- Invite children who investigate the natural items in the Discovery area to share what they observed.

Investigation 5

What are balls made of?

	Day 1	Day 2	Day 3
Interest Areas	Art: thin strips (1–2 inches wide) of newspaper or paper towels; glue; water; balloons	Art: thin strips (1–2 inches wide) of newspaper or paper towels; glue; water; balloons Discovery: balls that can and cannot be opened	Art: thin strips (1–2 inches wide) of newspaper or paper towels; glue; water; balloons Discovery: balls that can and cannot be opened
Question of the Day	Can you make a ball?	What do you think is inside these balls?	Do you think a bubble is a ball?
Large Group	Movement: move like a balloon Discussion and Shared Writing: Using Our Senses to Explore Balls Materials: Mighty Minutes 39, "Let's Pretend"; container with balls made of different materials	Song: "We Like Clapping" Discussion and Shared Writing: What Do You Think Is Inside a Ball? Materials: Mighty Minutes 89, "We Like Clapping"; ball collection	Game: My Name, Too! Discussion and Shared Writing: Hollow and Solid Materials: inflated beach ball; beach ball filled with sand; Mighty Minutes 35, "My Name, Too!"
Read-Aloud	*The Doorbell Rang*	*A Birthday Basket for Tía*	*The Doorbell Rang*
Small Group	Option 1: Walk a Letter Intentional Teaching Card LL17, "Walk a Letter"; masking tape; alphabet cards or chart Option 2: Jumping Beans Intentional Teaching Card LL05, "Jumping Beans"; construction paper; marker; scissors; lamination supplies or clear contact paper; coffee can	Option 1: Rhyming Riddles Intentional Teaching Card LL11, "Rhyming Riddles"; props that rhyme with chosen words Option 2: Rhyming Names Intentional Teaching Card LL10, "Rhyming Chart"; chart paper; marker; poem or song with rhymes; props that illustrate the song or poem; Intentional Teaching Card LL19, "Silly Names"	Option 1: What Happened Next? Intentional Teaching Card LL01, "Shared Writing" Option 2: Continuing the Story Intentional Teaching Card LL04, "Bookmaking"; cardboard or card stock; paper; crayons, pencils or markers; bookbinding supplies
Mighty Minutes™	Mighty Minutes 19, "I Spy With My Little Eye"	Mighty Minutes 38, "Spatial Patterns"	Mighty Minutes 41, "The Imaginary Ball"; numeral cards

Day 4	Day 5	Make Time For...
Art: completed papier mâché balls; collection of spheres and circles	Art: completed papier mâché balls; collection of spheres and circles; Intentional Teaching Card LL26, "Searching the Web"	### Outdoor Experiences
Discovery: deflated balls; pumps		**Exploring Bubbles**
Computer: eBook version of *Have a Ball*	Computers: Web sites that answer questions about what's inside balls	• Bring some bubble solution and wands outside for the children to explore.
What ball-shaped food do you like best?	Can this ball be opened?	• Ask, "Is a bubble a ball?"

• Ask, "Why is a bubble always round even if you use a square wand?" |
| Song: "We Like Clapping" | Game: I Spy... | • Ask, "How are bubbles the same as or different from other types of balls?" |
| **Discussion and Shared Writing:** Ball-Shaped Foods | **Discussion and Shared Writing:** Finding Answers | • Record the children's ideas and take pictures of their investigation. |
| **Materials:** Mighty Minutes 89, "We Like Clapping"; music; Mighty Minutes 43, "Bouncing Big Brown Balls" | **Materials:** Mighty Minutes 19, "I Spy With My Little Eye"; balls that can't be opened | **Physical Fun**

• Review Intentional Teaching Card P25, "Kick Hard." Follow the guidance on the card. |
| *Have a Ball* paper; markers | *The Doorbell Rang* set of 12 counters or other manipulatives | ### Family Partnerships

• Invite families to participate in the end-of-study celebration. |
Option 1: Making Play Dough	**Option 1: Dinnertime**	
Intentional Teaching Card M15, "Play Dough" (See card for equipment, ingredients, and recipe.)	Intentional Teaching Card M01, "Dinnertime"; paper or plastic dishes; utensils; napkins; cups; placemats	
Option 2: Matzo Balls	**Option 2: Number Cards**	
Intentional Teaching Card M24, "Matzo Balls" (See card for equipment, ingredients, and recipe.)	Intentional Teaching Card M04, "Number Cards"; set of numeral cards with a numeral and its number word printed on one side; buttons or other small manipulatives	
Mighty Minutes 24, "Dinky Doo"	Mighty Minutes 25, "Freeze"; dance music; alphabet cards	

Investigation 5

What are balls made of?

Vocabulary

English: *senses*

Spanish: *los sentidos*

Large Group

Opening Routine

- Sing a welcome song and talk about who's here.

Movement: Move Like a Balloon

- Review Mighty Minutes 39, "Let's Pretend." Follow the guidance on the card.

Discussion and Shared Writing: Using Our Senses to Explore Balls

- Gather several balls made of different materials, e.g. a rubber ball, hollow plastic ball, leather or vinyl football, Styrofoam™ ball, yarn ball, rubber band ball, cotton ball, golf ball, clay or dough ball, beach ball.

- Say, "Sometimes we can figure things out by using our *senses*. What senses can we use to try to find out what these balls are made of?" Encourage the children to include words such as *listen, smell, taste, touch,* and *look* in their responses.

- Put one ball at a time in a mystery bag or box. Give each child a chance to put a hand in the bag, use his or her sense of touch, and describe the way the ball feels.

- Take the ball out and pass it around for each child to feel. Repeat this experience with other balls.

- Record children's descriptive words.

Before transitioning to interest areas, refer to the question of the day. Talk about the balloons and papier mâché in the Art area and how children can use them to make a ball.

Choice Time

As you interact with children in the interest areas, make time to

- Offer guidance as children use the papier mâché. Say, "Dip the paper in the glue mixture, and then pull the paper between two fingers to get all the extra glue off."

- Ask open-ended questions to encourage children to think and respond, e.g., "What does the papier mâché feel like?"

- Record what children say and do.

Read-Aloud

Read *The Doorbell Rang.*

- **Before you read**, tell the children the title of the book. Ask, "What do you think this book will be about?"

- **As you read**, pause each time after you say, "The doorbell rang," and ask the children to predict what will happen next.

- **After you read**, point out that the word *doorbell* is a compound word. Say the word *doorbell* slowly. Ask, "Can you tell me what two words you hear when I say the word *doorbell*?"

English-language learners
When reading the phrase "the doorbell rang," pantomime ringing a doorbell or ring a bell. Combining actions with words helps all children understand and learn vocabulary.

Small Group

Option 1: Walk a Letter

- Review Intentional Teaching Card LL17, "Walk a Letter." Follow the guidance on the card.

Option 2: Jumping Beans

- Review Intentional Teaching Card LL05, "Jumping Beans." Follow the guidance on the card.

See *The Creative Curriculum for Preschool, Volume 3: Literacy* for more information on supporting children's alphabet knowledge.

Mighty Minutes™

- Use Mighty Minutes 19, "I Spy With My Little Eye." Follow the guidance on the card.

- Try the shape variation on the back.

Large-Group Roundup

- Recall the day's events.

- Encourage children who used papier mâché during choice time to talk about their experiences.

- Ask the children to help you make a sign for the classroom inviting families to the end-of-study celebration.

What are balls made of?

Vocabulary

English: *hollow, solid*

Spanish: *hueca, compacta*

Large Group

Opening Routine

- Sing a welcome song and talk about who's here.

Song: "We Like Clapping"

- Review Mighty Minutes 89, "We Like Clapping." Follow the guidance on the card.

Discussion and Shared Writing: What Do You Think Is Inside a Ball?

- Say, "We were able to use our sense of touch to feel the outside of a ball and talk about what it is made of on the outside. But what do you think is inside a ball?"

- Record children's answers. Introduce the words *hollow* and *solid*. Show objects that allow the children to see a hollow inside and a solid inside.

- Refer to the question of the day.

- Show the children the collection of balls.

- Ask the children to predict whether each ball is hollow or solid. Sort the balls accordingly.

Before transitioning to interest areas, tell the children that they may check their predictions in the Discovery area by helping you cut open old balls.

Choice Time

As you interact with children in the interest areas, make time to

- Help children open old balls in the Discovery area.

- Invite children to sort the balls by what is inside them. Suggest including a "balls we can't open" category. Help children make labels for each category.

- Continue to assist children as they work with the papier mâché in the Art area.

- Record what children say and do.

Use your knowledge of the children in your class to determine when they can safely do something by themselves. If you think that they're not quite ready, have them help or watch you do it. In either case, be sure to offer verbal support and suggestions.

Read-Aloud

Read *A Birthday Basket for Tía.*

- **Before you read**, tell the children the title of the book, and show the cover. Ask, "What do you think might be in Tía's birthday basket?"

- **As you read**, write on chart paper the name of each gift that Cecilia puts in the basket.

- **After you read**, review the list of gifts. Ask, "What made each gift special? What would you put in a birthday basket for your tía?"

Small Group

Option 1: Rhyming Riddles

- Review Intentional Teaching Card LL11, "Rhyming Riddles." Follow the guidance on the card, using *balls* as the topic.

Option 2: Rhyming Names

- Review Intentional Teaching Card LL10, "Rhyming Chart." Follow the guidance on the card.

- See Intentional Teaching Card LL19 "Silly Names." Read the poem "Laughing Leo" aloud. Ask, "What if, instead of *starting* with the same sound, Leo's name *ended* with the same sound?"

- Invite the children to generate new rhyming names for Laughing Leo and for themselves.

Mighty Minutes™

- Use Mighty Minutes 38, "Spatial Patterns." Follow the guidance on the card.

Large-Group Roundup

- Recall the day's events.

- Invite children who explored the inside of balls during choice time to describe what they learned.

Day 3 | Investigation 5

What are balls made of?

Vocabulary

English: *hollow, solid*

Spanish: *hueca, compacta*

Large Group

Opening Routine

- Sing a welcome song and talk about who's here.

Game: My Name, Too!

- Review Mighty Minutes 35, "My Name, Too!" Follow the guidance on the card, using the beginning sounds of names.

Discussion and Shared Writing: Hollow and Solid

- Examine the documentation from yesterday about *hollow* and *solid* balls. Ask, "Why do you think some balls are solid and some balls are hollow? How would a ball that is hollow move differently if it were solid?"

- Show an example of an inflated beach ball and a beach ball filled with sand. (Use a funnel to fill with sand.) Ask, "How are these balls the same? How are they different?"

- Have pairs of children roll, kick, bounce, and throw hollow and solid balls. Encourage them to notice any differences between those experiences.

- Discuss and record children's discoveries.

- Refer to the question of the day. Ask, "What is inside a bubble?"

Before transitioning to interest areas, tell the children that they may continue to help you cut open old balls in the Discovery area to see what is inside them.

Choice Time

As you interact with children in the interest areas, make time to

- Help children open balls in the Discovery area.

- Encourage children to sort the balls into the categories from the day before and count the number of balls in each category. Ask, "Which group has more balls? Which has fewer balls?"

- Continue to help children as they work with the papier mâché in the Art area.

- Record what children say and do.

Read-Aloud

Read *The Doorbell Rang*.

- **Before you read**, ask, "Who can remember what this book is about?"

- **As you read**, pause to let children fill in predictable, repeated phrases.

- **After you read**, ask the children to recall a time when they shared something. Invite them to talk about their experiences.

Small Group

Option 1: What Happened Next?

- Review Intentional Teaching Card LL01, "Shared Writing." Follow the guidance on the card.

- Ask children to recall the end of *The Doorbell Rang*.

- Ask, "Who do you think was there?"

Option 2: Continuing the Story

- Review Intentional Teaching Card LL04, "Bookmaking." Follow the guidance on the card.

- Ask children to recall the end of *The Doorbell Rang*.

- Ask, "Who do you think was there?"

Mighty Minutes™

- Use Mighty Minutes 41, "The Imaginary Ball." Follow the guidance on the card.

- Try the number variation on the back of the card.

Large-Group Roundup

- Recall the day's events.

- Invite children who sorted balls in the Discovery area to talk about the number of balls in each category. Ask, "Which category had the most balls? Which had the fewest?"

What are balls made of?

Vocabulary

English: *sculpture*

Spanish: *escultura*

Large Group

Opening Routine

- Sing a welcome song and talk about who's here.

Song: "We Like Clapping"

- Review Mighty Minutes 89, "We Like Clapping." Follow the guidance on the card playing fast and slow music.

> You can use recorded music or you can play your own fast and slow music on a guitar, drum, keyboard, or tambourine.

Discussion and Shared Writing: Ball-Shaped Foods

- Review the question of the day.

- Ask, "What other foods can you think of that are shaped like a ball?"

- Record the children's responses.

- Review Mighty Minutes 43, "Bouncing Big Brown Balls." Follow the guidance on the card and create verses about ball-shaped foods.

Before transitioning to interest areas, talk about the materials in the Art area that children can use to create ball sculptures. Tell them that they may use their papier mâché balls and other kinds of spheres and circles collected throughout the study. Also show the children the deflated balls and pumps in the Discovery area and talk about how they can use them.

> The papier mâché balls must be completely dry before children put paint and glue on them. You can use a hairdryer to speed up the drying process.

Choice Time

As you interact with children in the interest areas, make time to

- Ask children about their artwork and their sculpting process. "Can you tell me about your sculpture? What will you add next?"

- Observe children as they work with the pumps and deflated balls in the Discovery area. Point out that inflating a ball is much easier when they work together, e.g., one person holds the ball while the other pumps.

- Record what children say and do.

English-language learners
This ball-inflation activity provides an excellent opportunity for English-language learners and English-speaking children to work together because it does not require verbal skills.

Read-Aloud

Read *Have a Ball.*

- **Before you read**, ask, "Who can remember what this book is about?"

- **As you read**, encourage children to add what they now know about the concepts in the book.

- **After you read**, give the children paper and markers so they can create a new page of the book. Encourage them to depict something they've learned during the balls study. Tell the children that the book will be available to them on the computer in the Computer area.

Small Group

Option 1: Making Play Dough

- Review Intentional Teaching Card M15, "Play Dough." Follow the guidance on the card.

- Encourage children to use the play dough to create different sizes of balls. Make comments that encourage them to compare the balls, e.g., "I wonder how we could line these up. Which ball do you think is the heaviest?"

Option 2: Making Matzo Balls

- Review Intentional Teaching Card M24, "Matzo Balls." Follow the guidance on the card.

Mighty Minutes™

- Use Mighty Minutes 24, "Dinky Doo." Follow the guidance on the card.

Large-Group Roundup

- Recall the day's events.

- Invite children who worked on their ball sculptures during choice time to share their work.

Day 5   Investigation 5

What are balls made of?

Vocabulary

English: *sphere, circle*

Spanish: *esfera, círculo*

Large Group

Opening Routine

- Sing a welcome song and talk about who's here.

Game: I Spy…

- Review Mighty Minutes 19, "I Spy With My Little Eye."

- Try the shape variation on the back of the card, using circles and spheres.

Discussion and Shared Writing: Finding Answers

- Talk about the question of the day.

- Remind the children about the experience from the other day in which they sorted balls into a "balls we can't open" category.

- Show them a marble and bowling ball (or other balls you can't open). Say, "We couldn't find out what was inside these balls because we couldn't cut them open."

- Ask, "If we want to find out something that we don't know, what are some ways we can find out?" Record their responses.

- Review the questions that children generated about balls throughout the study. Point out which ones have not yet been answered as a result of their investigations.

Before transitioning to interest areas, tell children that they can use the computers to find some of the answers to the unanswered questions. Also point out that the materials for making ball sculptures are still available for them to use in the Art area.

Choice Time

As you interact with children in the interest areas, make time to

- Guide their exploration of the Internet to find the answers to their questions.

- Continue to help children as they work with the papier mâché in the Art area.

- Record what children say and do.

> **See Intentional Teaching Card LL26, "Searching the Web" for more information.**

Read-Aloud

Read *The Doorbell Rang*.

- **Before you read**, ask, "What is the name of this book?"

- **As you read**, pause occasionally and encourage children to retell the story.

- **After you read**, show the children a set of 12 counters or other manipulatives. Tell them that they will re-create the story and use the manipulatives as cookies. Invite the children to retell the story and act out the parts of Victoria, Sam, and their visitors. Have the children help you divide the manipulatives among the characters as the story unfolds.

English-language learners
Predictable books with simple text and a lot of repetition are particularly effective in helping children increase their vocabularies and comprehension.

Small Group

Option 1: Dinnertime

- Review Intentional Teaching Card M01, "Dinnertime." Follow the guidance on the card.

Option 2: Number Cards

- Review Intentional Teaching Card M04, "Number Cards." Follow the guidance on the card.

See *The Creative Curriculum for Preschool, Volume 4: Mathematics* for more information on supporting children's use of number concepts and operations.

Mighty Minutes™

- Use Mighty Minutes 25, "Freeze."

- Try the letter variation on the back of the card.

Large-Group Roundup

- Recall the day's events.

- Encourage children who researched their unanswered questions about balls on the Internet to share what they learned.

Further Questions to Investigate

If children are still engaged in this study and want to find out more, you might investigate additional questions. Here are some suggestions:

- Which balls can I throw, kick, or roll the farthest?

- What happens when you put a ball in the freezer? Will it bounce higher?

- How do basketball players spin balls on their fingers?

- What kinds of balls do different pets like?

- What kinds of ball games do children in other communities play?

- Can balls be used as decorations?

Are there additional questions that will help you extend this study?

Our Investigation

Our Investigation

	Day 1	Day 2	Day 3
Interest Areas			
Question of the Day			
Large Group			
Read-Aloud			
Small Group			
Mighty Minutes™			

Day 4	Day 5	Make Time For...
		Outdoor Experiences
		Family Partnerships
		Wow! Experiences

Our Investigation

Vocabulary

English:

Spanish:

Large Group

Choice Time

Read-Aloud

Small Group

Mighty Minutes™

Large-Group
Roundup

Celebrating Learning

Closing the Study

When the study ends—when most of the children's questions have been answered—it is important to reflect and celebrate. Plan a special way to celebrate their learning and accomplishments. Allow children to assume as much responsibility as possible for planning the activities. Here are some suggestions:

- Set up stations for children to show visitors how they investigated balls.

- Host an Olympics in which children can play various ball games.

- Have the children plan a meal featuring foods shaped like balls, such as oranges, cheese balls, sherbet balls, olives, meatballs, and matzo balls. Invite family members to participate.

- Invite families to an informal picnic featuring ball games and ball-shaped foods.

- Invent a new ball game, and teach it to the children in another class.

- Make a class book, photo album, documentation panel, or slide show about the ball study.

- Record a video of children demonstrating what they learned and interviewing each other about balls. Show the video to the children's families.

Celebrating Learning

	Day 1	Day 2	
Interest Areas	All: displays of children's investigations Computer: eBook version of *The Little Red Hen*	All: displays of children's investigations Computer: eBook version of *Play Ball!*	
Question of the Day	Tomorrow, what would you like to show our guests at the celebration about the balls study?	What was your favorite part of the balls study?	
Large Group	**Movement:** The Imaginary Ball **Discussion and Shared Writing:** Preparing for the Celebration **Materials:** Mighty Minutes 41, "The Imaginary Ball"; numeral cards	**Poem:** "Come Play With Me" **Discussion and Shared Writing:** Sharing Special Foods **Materials:** Mighty Minutes 42, "Come Play With Me"; ball-shaped foods	
Read-Aloud	*The Little Red Hen* markers; chart paper	*Play Ball!*	
Small Group	**Option 1: Show Me Five** Intentional Teaching Card M16, "Show Me Five"; collection of marbles, buttons, seeds, etc. **Option 2: Nursery Rhyme Count** Intentional Teaching Card M13, "Nursery Rhyme Count"; cotton balls; green construction paper; numeral cards	**Option 1: Recounting the Ball Collection** Intentional Teaching Card M06, "Tallying"; clipboard; paper; pencils or crayons **Option 2: Voting** Intentional Teaching Card M06, "Tallying"; clipboard; paper; pencils or crayons	
Mighty Minutes™	Mighty Minutes 24, "Dinky Doo"	Mighty Minutes 30, "Bounce, Bounce, Bounce"	

Make Time For...

Outdoor Experiences

Physical Fun

- Use Intentional Teaching Card P04, "Kick High."
  Follow the guidance on the card.

Family Partnerships

- Include families in the celebration.
- Invite families to access the eBook, *The Little Red Hen.*

Wow! Experiences

- Day 2: Balls celebration

Celebrating Learning

Let's plan our celebration

Vocabulary

English: *poem*

Spanish: *poema*

Large Group

Opening Routine

- Sing a welcome song and talk about who's here.

Movement: The Imaginary Ball

- Review Mighty Minutes 41, "The Imaginary Ball." Follow the guidance on the card.

Discussion and Shared Writing: Preparing for the Celebration

- Talk about the celebration tomorrow.

- Remind the children about the question of the day.

- Ask the children what they want to show families and guests about what they learned during the study. Make a list of their responses.

Before transitioning to interest areas, tell children that you will help them gather the items from the list to create displays for family and friends to see at tomorrow's celebration.

Choice Time

As you interact with children in the interest areas, make time to

- Help children gather the items they would like to share at the celebration.

Read-Aloud

Read *The Little Red Hen.*

- **Before you read**, ask, "What happens in this story?"

- **As you read**, pause to encourage children to retell the events of the story. Ask, "What does the little red hen do next?"

- **After you read**, point out that lines of text from several pages are repeated at the end as a poem. Write the poem on chart paper. Reread the poem and encourage the children to notice the rhyming words. Underline them. Read it again, and pause to let the children fill in the alternating rhyming words. Tell the children that the book will be available to them on the computer in the Computer area.

Small Group

Option 1: Show Me Five

- Review Intentional Teaching Card M16, "Show Me Five." Follow the guidance on the card.

Option 2: Nursery Rhyme Count

- Review Intentional Teaching Card M13, "Nursery Rhyme Count." Follow the guidance on the card.

Mighty Minutes™

- Use Mighty Minutes 24, "Dinky Doo." Follow the guidance on the card.

Large-Group Roundup

- Recall the day's events.

- Remind the children that there will be a special celebration tomorrow.

For more ideas about closing the study, see *The Creative Curriculum for Preschool, Volume 1: The Foundation,* Chapter 3.

Day 2 — Celebrating Learning

Let's celebrate

Vocabulary

English: *tally*

Spanish: *llevar la cuenta*

Large Group

Opening Routine

- Sing a welcome song and talk about who's here.

Poem: "Come Play With Me"

- Review Mighty Minutes 42, "Come Play With Me." Follow the guidance on the card.

Discussion and Shared Writing: Sharing Special Foods

- Invite family members who brought ball-shaped foods to describe them.

- Record the names of the foods. Point out any names that are compound words. Say each word slowly and encourage the children to identify the two words that make up the compound word.

- Review the question of the day.

Before transitioning to interest areas, talk about the displays of children's learning that you've set up around the room and the ball games to play outside.

Choice Time

As you interact with children in the interest areas, make time to

- Invite the children to explain to the visitors what they've learned about balls. Use the displays as prompts.

Read-Aloud

Read *Play Ball!*

- **Before you read**, ask, "Who remembers the name of this book?"

- **As you read**, pause and allow children to fill in rhyming words.

- **After you read**, encourage children to relate the balls and games in the book to their many experiences during the balls study. Tell the children that the book will be available to them on the computer in the Computer area.

Small Group

Option 1: Recounting the Ball Collection

- Review Intentional Teaching Card M06, "Tallying."

- Follow the guidance on the card to count the ball collection.

Option 2: Voting

- Guide the children as they generate a list of major events from the study, e.g., playing with balls outside, visiting the store, and the pet visit.

- Review Intentional Teaching Card M06, "Tallying."

- Follow the guidance on the card. Have the children interview each other and record the votes for their favorite part of the study.

Mighty Minutes™

- Use Mighty Minutes 30, "Bounce, Bounce, Bounce." Follow the guidance on the card.

Large-Group Roundup

- Recall the day's events.

- Talk about how much children learned during the study by briefly reviewing the displays related to the investigations.

Reflecting on the Study

What were the most engaging parts of the study?

Are there other topics that might be worth investigating?

If I were to change any part of the study, it would be:

Other thoughts and ideas I have:

Resources

Background Information for Teachers

Among other phenomena, physical science explores energy, force, and the way objects move. Because balls bounce, spin, and roll in all directions and also store and transfer energy, exploring balls is a way to learn physical science concepts. Most balls are spheres, which means that they look like a circle from every angle.

Mass is the amount of matter an object contains. For example, a piece of foil has the same mass whether it is a flat sheet or rolled into a ball.

Momentum is the strength of an object's motion. The amount of strength depends on the ball's mass and velocity (speed). A ball has more momentum the faster it is thrown. A ball with more mass, rolling at the same speed as a ball with less mass, also has more momentum.

Gravity is the natural force that pulls things to or near a heavenly body's surface, such as Earth's, to its center. That is why a ball falls to the ground when you drop it.

Galileo was the first to demonstrate that objects fall at the same rate of speed regardless of their size. It is said that he dropped two objects of different masses from the Tower of Pisa, and they landed on the ground at the same time.

Lightweight falling objects, such as feathers and ping-pong balls, are slowed by air resistance and therefore do not fall at the same rate of speed as heavier objects.

The weight of an object is the force of gravity pulling on the object. It varies with the mass of the object and the strength of gravity.

Energy is the ability to do work or to move an object. A moving ball has kinetic energy. For a ball to move, force must be applied to it, e.g., in the form of a throw, push, or pull.

Friction is a force that resists motion when two things come in contact with one another, e.g., rub against or touch each other. A moving ball is slowed by friction whenever the ball touches something else, such as grass, sand, water, or air.

Several forces are involved when a ball is thrown. The ball is sent forward by the force of the throw, pulled down by gravity, and slowed by air resistance.

A ball will rebound when you drop it onto a hard surface. However, it will not bounce back to its starting position because the force of friction slows it down.

Vocabulary: *mass, momentum, gravity, weight, energy, friction, velocity*

What do you want to research to help you understand this topic?

Children's Books

In addition to the children's books specifically used in this *Teaching Guide*, you may wish to supplement daily activities and interest areas with some of the listed children's books.

Balls! (Michael J. Rosen)

Balls! Elmo's World (John E. Barrett and Mary Beth Nelson)

Beach Ball (Peter Sis)

Curious George Plays Baseball (Margaret Rey)

Froggy Plays Soccer (Jonathan London)

Froggy Plays T-Ball (Jonathan London)

Hit the Ball, Duck! (Jez Alborough)

Joey and Jet (James Yang)

Kids Around the World Play! The Best Fun and Games from Many Lands (Arlette Braman)

Play Ball (Mercer Mayer)

Play Ball, Amelia Bedelia (Peggy Parish)

Players in Pigtails (Shana Corey)

Roll, Slope, and Slide: A Book About Ramps (Michael Dahl)

Round Like a Ball (Lisa Campbell Ernst)

Snowballs (Lois Ehlert)

Stop That Ball (Mike McClintock)

The Ball Book (Margaret Hillert)

The Giant Ball of String (Arthur Geisert)

The Lost Ball / La pelota perdida (Lynn Reiser)

The Matzo Ball Boy (Lisa Shulman)

The Snowy Day (Ezra Jack Keats)

The Story of Red Rubber Ball (Constance Kling Levy)

The Three Magic Balls (Richard Egielski)

Watch Me Throw the Ball (Mo Willems)

Winnie Plays Ball (Leda Schubert)

Teacher Resources

The teacher resources provide additional information and ideas for enhancing and extending the study topic.

Balls (Melanie Davis Jones)

Baseball ABC and Baseball 123 (DK Publishing)

Bouncing Science: No-Sweat Projects (Jess Brallier)

Goal! My Soccer Book; Touchdown! My Football Book; Slam Dunk! My Basketball Book; Home Run! My Baseball Book (David Diehl)

H is for Home Run: A Baseball Alphabet; J is for Jump Shot: A Basketball Alphabet; K is for Kick: A Soccer Alphabet; P is for Putt: A Golf Alphabet; T is for Touchdown: A Football Alphabet (Brad Herzog)

My Basketball Book; My Football Book; My Soccer Book (Gail Gibbons)

This Is Baseball (Margaret Blackstone)

Weekly Planning Form

Week of: _____   Teacher: _____   Study: _____

	Monday	Tuesday	Wednesday	Thursday	Friday
Interest Areas					
Large Group					
Read-Aloud					
Small Group					

Outdoor Experiences:

Family Partnerships:

Wow! Experiences:

Weekly Planning Form, continued

"To-Do" List:

Reflecting on the week:

Individual Child Planning